YoungWriters 2006 Poetry Comp

'I have a dream that my children will one day live in a nation where they will not be judged by the color of their skin, but by the content of their character.'

Martin Luther King

I have a dream

words to change the world

- **MOTIVATE** your pupils to write and appreciate poetry.
- **INSPIRE** them to share their hopes and dreams for the future.
- **BOOST** awareness of your school's creative ability.
- **WORK** alongside the National Curriculum or the high level National Qualification Skills.
- Supports the *Every Child Matters - Make a Positive Contribution* outcome.
- Over £7,000 of great prizes for schools and pupils.

'When I was out there I was never ever alone, there was always a team of people behind me, in mind if not in body.'
Ellen MacArthur

South East England
Edited by Heather Killingray

Young Writers

First published in Great Britain in 2006 by:
Young Writers
Remus House
Coltsfoot Drive
Peterborough
PE2 9JX
Telephone: 01733 890066
Website: www.youngwriters.co.uk

SB ISBN 1 84602 522 2

Foreword

Imagine a teenager's brain; a fertile yet fragile expanse teeming with ideas, aspirations, questions and emotions. Imagine a classroom full of racing minds, scratching pens writing an endless stream of ideas and thoughts . . .

. . . Imagine your words in print reaching a wider audience. Imagine that maybe, just maybe, your words can make a difference. Strike a chord. Touch a life. Change the world. Imagine no more . . .

'I Have a Dream' is a series of poetry collections written by 11 to 18-year-olds from schools and colleges across the UK and overseas. Pupils were invited to send us their poems using the theme 'I Have a Dream'. Selected entries range from dreams they've experienced to childhood fantasies of stardom and wealth, through inspirational poems of their dreams for a better future and of people who have influenced and inspired their lives.

The series is a snapshot of who and what inspires, influences and enthuses young adults of today. It shows an insight into their hopes, dreams and aspirations of the future and displays how their dreams are an escape from the pressures of today's modern life. Young Writers are proud to present this anthology, which is truly inspired and sure to be an inspiration to all who read it.

Contents

Charters School, Ascot

Lee Perrett (13)	58
Sophie Drake (14)	58

The Downs School, Newbury

Helen Gardner (13)	59
Luke Griffiths (16)	59
Alice Malthouse (13)	60
Nicole Rumble (14)	61
Camilla Chichester (12)	62
Courtney Holmes (12)	62
Matt Northfield (12)	63
Charley New (13)	63
Joni Richardson (13)	64
Emilia Ramirez (13)	64
David Seymour (13)	65
Charlotte MacRae (12)	65
Tom Wigg (13)	66
Emma Daniel (12)	67
Libby Hordos (13)	68
Chris Abbott (13)	69
Ashleigh Evans (13)	70
Joe Davies (13)	70
Katy Waters (13)	71
Sophie Preece (12)	72
Helen Booker (13)	73
Stephanie Brown (12)	74
Sarah Tranter (14)	75
Eleanor Bunn (13)	75
Caroline Pringle (15)	76
Emma Hounsell (13)	76
John Morgan (12)	77
Grace Ladds (14)	78
Katy Burgess (12)	79
Josh Dickins (15)	80
Jamie Pincott (16)	81
Robert Taylor (15)	81
Tom Meredith (13)	82
Josh Overton (16)	82
Katherine Browne (13)	83
Nancy Leadley (14)	84
Stacy Mills (13)	85

Windsor Girls' School, Windsor

The Poems

I Have A Dream

I have a dream that there will be no one who is racist.
I have a dream that everyone will be honest with each other.
I have a dream to change the way people express their own
                                    opinions behind people's backs,
So they could be said to their faces.
I have a dream that violence will stop in the streets.
I have a dream that nobody should be scared of his or her
                                    own environment.
I have a dream that nobody would be insecure about himself
                                    or herself.
I have a dream that there will be peace in the world.
I have a dream that children could feel safe about not being beaten
                                    or abused.
I have a dream that all people should be treated the same way.
I have a dream that there can be world peace.
I have a dream that there will be no more break ups.
I have a dream that relationships could never be broken.
I have a dream that people would never go behind people's backs
                                    and betray other people.
I have a dream that people would be safe wherever they go.
I have a dream that good things would always happen to everyone
                                    in the world.
I have a dream that relationships would last forever.

Liam Chute (14)
Bensham Manor School, Thornton Heath

I Have A Dream

I have a dream I want to be a dancer.
I have a dream to meet Dick and Dom and Tracy.
I have a dream to be a nursery teacher.
I have a dream to swim with dolphins.
I have a dream to be a good swimmer.

Sarah Wright (12)
Bensham Manor School, Thornton Heath

I Have A Dream

I have a dream to move on to college
and study art, film and music.

I have a dream to be a film director.

I have a dream to settle down and have
a wife and children.

I have a dream to move my mum and
dad into a mansion.

I have a dream to see my friends
prosper in life.

I have a dream to be involved in music.

I have a dream that me and my friends
will be well known.

I have a dream to see my sister prosper in life as well.

Dean Rice (15)
Bensham Manor School, Thornton Heath

I Have A Dream

I have a dream to work towards
becoming a great story writer and animator.
I have a dream to travel all over the world
and to visit many places.
I have a dream to marry someone
and have good children.
I have a dream to live long.
I have a dream that mankind
can remove war and poverty
and will blast off to the stars.

Laurence O'Hara (14)
Bensham Manor School, Thornton Heath

I Have A Dream

I have a dream that I will become a prefect
in my last year at school.
I have a dream to be famous for
creating a new computer game.
I have a dream to become a footballer
and play for England.
I have a dream to become an ICT teacher.
I have a dream to do IT courses at college.
I have a dream that I will visit the other
nine planets with Mr Novak and Mr Kemp.
I have a dream that I will become famous
for scoring a goal for England's football team.

Aadil Sumar (14)
Bensham Manor School, Thornton Heath

I Have A Dream

I have a dream that I want to be a pop star
because I want to sing and be inside magazines.
I want people to vote for me.
I want to have a good single.
I want to win and go in all different competitions.
I have a dream to be an artist because I am good at art.
I want to be the best at drawing in the whole world.
I have a dream that I will work with children.
I get pleasure from helping children.
I help some children read and write.
I have a dream that I will meet Blazin' Squad.
I want to get their photos and autographs.
I will ask them out and give them my number.
I have a dream that I want to be a good writer.
I want to make my own story and rhyming words.

Zoya Tyrrell Walters (16)
Bensham Manor School, Thornton Heath

I Have A Dream

I have a dream that I will become rich and famous.
I have a dream that I will be a singer and an actress one day.
I have a dream of doing dancing in the 'Christmas
Entertainment Production 2006'.
I have a dream that I will take a ride in a new limousine,
just like in 'America's Next Top Model'.
I have a dream of getting married to a mysterious handsome man.
I have a dream to have kids.
I have a dream of moving to a new house in Hollywood.
I have a dream of being best mates with Lesley.
I have a dream of being best mates with Kieran for all my life.
I have a dream that I will dance with my dance partner
in 'Strictly Come Dancing'.
I have a dream of seeing Jesse McCartney (don't tell everyone!).
I have a dream to change my room from cream to gold for my
                                            14th birthday.
I have a dream to have pink and lilac furniture, with a silver ceiling
                                    and a gold wardrobe.
I have a dream that everyone will know my name.

Chloe Knight (13)
Bensham Manor School, Thornton Heath

I Have A Dream

I have a dream that they will build a high fence in the playground.
I have a dream of getting married to a beautiful woman.
I have a dream of looking at the planets.
I have a dream that there will be no more wars.
I have a dream of travelling independently to school.
I have a dream of being a part-time actor.
I have a dream about girls.
I have a dream that I will write books.

Matthew Hagon (14)
Bensham Manor School, Thornton Heath

I Have A Dream . . .

I have a dream of world peace, where there will be no fighting and
conflict, hate and war, for the world to live peacefully.
I have a dream that animal cruelty will stop and
abandoning animals will stop.
I have a dream to be a singer, who's rich and
is named 'Heart-throb' by lots of girls.
I have a dream to meet and kiss Lindsay Lohan, Keira Knightley,
some of Girls Aloud, the Sugababes, and Sky from Neighbours
because they're all fit and gorgeous.
I have a dream to be an author like Jacqueline Wilson,
and to meet lots of my fans and sell lots of books.
I have a dream to have a wife and kids.
I have a dream to have a red Ferrari and a mansion.
I have a dream to be remembered as a kind and caring person.
I have a dream to be an actor and see my name up in lights.
I have a dream to give the poor money and a job.
I have a dream for racism to stop.
I have a dream that ChildLine, the children's charity,
will be able to have lots of money to fund more calls
so that children can get through to them
and talk to them about why they're upset and unhappy.
I have a dream for people to be treated the same
and not treated differently for who they are.

Jonathan Land (14)
Bensham Manor School, Thornton Heath

I Have A Dream

I have a dream that I am rich.
I have a dream that I am a soap star.
I have a dream that the world is safe.
I have a dream that I become a football player.
I have a dream that London is a good place.
I have a dream that I am playing for Arsenal.

Kyle Sinclair (15)
Bensham Manor School, Thornton Heath

I Have A Dream

I have a dream about a dogs' home.
I could rescue all the dogs.
I have a dream about feeding them
And taking them for walks.
I have a dream about being
An artist, painting pictures.
I have a dream that I could change the world,
I could stop the fighting and all the wars.

Melissa Russell (12)
Bensham Manor School, Thornton Heath

I Have A Dream

I have a dream to be 50 Cent.
I have a dream to be a football player.
I have a dream to be Ronaldiniho.
I have a dream to be famous.
I have a dream to have a limousine.
I have a dream to play for Arsenal.
I have a dream to be on EastEnders.

Aston Carpenter (11)
Bensham Manor School, Thornton Heath

I Have A Dream

I have a dream that I would meet 50 Cent.
I have a dream to have a million dollars.
I have a dream to be a famous rapper.
I have a dream that I will go out with Beyoncé.
I have a dream that I would play for Man United.
I have a dream that I drive a Lamborghini.

Alex Williams (11)
Bensham Manor School, Thornton Heath

I Have A Dream

I have a dream to see my Uncle Leon.
I have a dream to stop war.
I have a dream to have peace on Earth.
I have a dream to be a football star!
I have a dream to give money and a home to the poor.
I have a dream to have a good day at school.
I have a dream to meet McFly!
I have a dream to give blood.
I have a dream for my family to be happy.
I have a dream to swim in the Olympics.
I have a dream to help animals.
I have a dream to be me!

Laura Kane (14)
Bensham Manor School, Thornton Heath

I Have A Dream

I have a dream to meet Billy Joel,
I have a dream of playing for Arsenal,
I have a dream of being a drummer,
I have a dream of meeting Thierry Henry,
I have a dream of meeting my dad's mum.

Thomas Leiper (11)
Bensham Manor School, Thornton Heath

I Have A Dream

I have a dream to be a singer.
I have a dream to meet Dick and Dom.
I have a dream to meet Tracy Beaker.
I have a dream to meet Man United.
I have a dream to be a pop star.

Christopher Munkombwe (11)
Bensham Manor School, Thornton Heath

I Have A Dream

I have a dream
that I will become rich and famous.
I have a dream
that I will be friends with everyone.
I have a dream
that I will have a fantastic world when I grow up.
I have a dream
that I will stay best friends with Tara
for all my whole life.
I have a dream
that I will never leave this school.
I have a dream
that I will be brighter.
I have a dream
that I could bring my grandma back and my uncle, Cliff.
I have a dream
that I will win thousands of pounds.
I have a dream
that I could have a better education for myself.
I have a dream
that I could have more pets.
I have a dream
that Kevin will not be mean or horrible to Mrs Robinson.
I have a dream
that everyone would be nice to me.

Melissa Page (15)
Bensham Manor School, Thornton Heath

I Have A Dream

I have a dream that I am a Formula 1 driver for McLaren.
I have a dream that I will go out with Claire.
I have a dream that I will live with my mum.
I have a dream that I will be a Power Ranger.
I have a dream that I will be a policeman.
I have a dream that I will live forever.

Darren Milsted (16)
Bensham Manor School, Thornton Heath

I Have A Dream

I have a dream I want to be a football player like Cristiano Ronaldo.
I have a dream to be a policeman.
I have a dream to be 50 Cent.
I have a dream to be in the fire brigade.
I have a dream I will go out with Beyoncé.

Kelvin Jones (11)
Bensham Manor School, Thornton Heath

I Have A Dream

I have a dream to be an archaeologist
to find some dinosaur bones.
I have a dream to meet Atomic Kitten,
to sing with them.
I have a dream to be a school teacher to teach art.
I have a dream to swim with dolphins,
to feel dolphin skin.
I have a dream to be a dancer,
to be a famous ballerina.

Alison Keattch (11)
Bensham Manor School, Thornton Heath

I Have A Dream

I have a dream about the people in Africa
getting very strong and healthy.
I have a dream that everyone will
become very clever and work hard.
I have a dream that animals will stop
being poached by hunters for their ivory.
I have a dream that people will
stop being killed in the war.

Thomas Sullivan (12)
Bensham Manor School, Thornton Heath

I Have A Dream

I have a dream that I can fly around the world
so I can see places in the world.
I want to race with planes and fighters.
I have a dream that I can see places in France,
Germany and America and go on holiday to Australia.
In Australia I will enjoy the sun and have fun
and go to America to see the Empire State Building in New York,
then go to France to see the Eiffel Tower.
I have a dream to fly to the highest cloud in the world,
then go higher than places.
Go on a fighter jet, then look down on cities and towns.
I dream that I will fly higher than the world
to see the Empire State Building.
But if I do all these things, I want to tell you now,
my dream is to be very funny in the world.

Tomi Abdullhai (16)
Bensham Manor School, Thornton Heath

It's What Will Make Me A Star

When I was three I dreamt of sweets,
The lolly my mum promised me.

When I was five I dreamt of days out,
To the park, or zoo, or sea.

When I was ten I dreamt of money
To buy that toy that looked so great.

When I was twelve I dreamt of fame,
To be out partying really late.

As I got older my dreams, they changed,
They've brought me here this far.

Having something to aim for,
It's what will make me a star.

Sammy Smith (13)
Blenheim High School, Epsom

If Time Stood Still

If time stood still, what would you see?
Would you see the same as me?

Would you only see suffering and pain?
A world void of anything other than fear?
No happiness, love, kindness or gain?

Do you think that no one from below to above,
From here to the farthest reaches of our world,
Has been taunted considerably by the force of love?

If you looked, would you only feel the cold of the night
As the world stood silently still,
Yet ignore the beauty of the stars so bright?

I would choose to see past all sadness and despair
In this unique world of ours,
To see that even in the blackest of hearts, love remains there!

I would see the sun shining on high above,
Smiling down at our busy world,
And be thankful for hope and love.

If time stood still, what would you see?
In my dream, you see the same as me.

Lottie Crossfield (13)
Blenheim High School, Epsom

My Grandad

I have a dream that one day people will be able to fight cancer,
Because my grandad had cancer, but he died from cancer.
I wish that people could help people with cancer,
So no more people will die from cancer.
I know that people will die from it,
But people could do a charity for the people that need help.

Annabella Morris (11)
Blenheim High School, Epsom

In Another World

In another world,
People don't lie in fear of those angry murderers.

In another world,
People know when they go to sleep they will wake up alive.

In another world,
Soldiers don't exist.

In another world,
The only conflict is friendly.

In another world,
People can sit back and think.

In another world,
Mines don't litter the earth and seas.

In another world,
Everyone is free.

In another world,
Continents hold hands.

In another world,
There is peace.

In another world . . .

Martin Lay (13)
Blenheim High School, Epsom

My Dream

When I was five,
I always dreamed to be a pop star
And would have loads of money
To buy a fancy car.
On TV, I would always watch 'Pop Idol'
And I dreamed that I would be on.

Hassana Sesay (12)
Blenheim High School, Epsom

Help!

Help is what people need,
We help raise money so people can feed.
Pop stars visit places just to see,
They try to help target the key.

They go to see what life is like,
They see not a toy, no teddy or a bike,
They see children starved,
They look so thin, like they have been carved.

Help all the people less fortunate than us,
Then treat them with a great big fuss.
I have a dream that people can be free,
Free from their life so they can speak to me.

Natasha Nahrwold (13)
Blenheim High School, Epsom

Dancing Dreams

I go every Saturday and Thursday,
It keeps me on my feet.
When I'm finished I want to stay,
So I cling tight to the seat.
We are a big, happy fleet.

On a Saturday I twist and twirl,
My outfits do often change.
My tights are the colour of a pearl,
We all bring a lot of change,
As the sweets they sell are a range.

On Thursday our outfits are black,
The logo's a luminous pink.
We bring our poms in a backpack.
With the cheers we often have to think,
And we can't dance like a kitchen sink.

Leanne Smith (11)
Blenheim High School, Epsom

My Dream

When you are young you think, *what comes next in life?*
Will it be nursery, school, even work? Enjoy your childhood.
You dream of being a superstar, it might not come true, but you
                                                    are dreaming.

Dreaming from young will present you with more options.
When you're a kid, enjoy the moment,
As you grow older, life can be tough.
That's why you should never stop dreaming for what you want.

So while you're a kid, keep dreaming till you have to stop.
There is nothing better, just go for what you can.
Dreaming motivates me, what motivates you?

Sam Brown (12)
Blenheim High School, Epsom

I Have A Dream

I have a dream to be happy,
I have a dream to have fun,
I have a dream to be running in the sunshine,
I have a dream to splash in the blue sea.

I wish I could be happy.

I have a dream to be successful,
I have a dream to be good looking,
I have a dream to be honest,
I have a dream to be loving and caring.

I wish I could be happy.

I have a dream of a palace,
I have a dream to help people,
I have a dream to be kind,
I have a dream to be a star.

All I want is to be happy.

Christina Alcock (12)
Blenheim High School, Epsom

They Have Feelings Too You Know

It makes me happy to see
The deer prancing with glee,
Skipping in the fields out in the open air,
Playing with their families with not a care.

That is until the hunters come
And shoot them for selfish gain,
For where once stood living, happiness and fun,
Now lies a dead soul rotting in the sun.

Why can't people see
That everyone's feelings are the same?
Humans or animals, what difference does it make?
Love them, care for them, don't leave them in pain.

If animals could talk,
People wouldn't hurt them.
Just because they can't,
We think nothing of it, so we abuse them.

They want to live a long, happy life,
Just like human beings.
Why can't we accept that
And act as if they exist in this world for a true meaning?

Faye Castleman (13)
Blenheim High School, Epsom

To Have A Dream Is . . . To Be A PE Teacher

I dream of being a PE teacher.
I dream of teaching all sports.
I dream of teaching kids how to play.
I dream of being the best.
I dream of playing sport all day long.
I dream of teaching kids the best.
I dream of being a PE teacher.

Shane Downey (12)
Blenheim High School, Epsom

Every Girl's . . . 'I Have A Dream'

That boys would listen to what you say,
instead of watching your lips have fun all day.

That chocolate and sweets could be eaten,
without spending a lifetime on hips, is that cheatin'?

That money can be spent,
but reappears in your pocket.

That football doesn't cling to boys,
apart from anything, it's too much noise!

That everyone loved the colour pink,
even the prime minister, pink sink?

That girls will be girls and boys will be boys . . .
This is my dream, did it make you boys scream?

Lizzie Dart (13)
Blenheim High School, Epsom

The Greenhouse

A greenhouse sits in the sun all day,
Taking in heat that can't go away.
There are fumes inside this house made of glass,
Everyone knows about it, but they just walk past.

One day soon, the world will drown
And everyone's face will turn to a frown.
Help is the word that the world will cry,
But no one will listen, everyone will die.

If only the world had listened to the facts
And had worked harder, not just relaxed,
Then maybe the world won't die out so soon,
And it will live on, without pollution and fumes.

Matthew Billups (12)
Blenheim High School, Epsom

My Dream

When they're gone,
they never come back.
When they lie in their graves,
they never come back.
When I think,
they never come back.
When I pray,
they never come back.
Oh why, oh why did they die
when I was only young?
I wish I had another chance
to really get to know them,
oh why, oh why are they not here?
They're here in spirit,
that is not the same.
They're here in my heart,
that is not the same.
They're here in my head,
that is not the same.

My dream is I wish
my nan and grandad
were still here.

Grace Sundborg (12)
Blenheim High School, Epsom

I Have A Dream

I want to be as friendly as my rabbit,
He makes me happy when I am sad.
He nibbles wires, it's a habit,
So he makes me really mad.

He's cute,
He's funny,
He's my bunny,
I wish I was the same as my honey bunny.

Zoe Merrett (12)
Blenheim High School, Epsom

What Football Is All About To Me

I love to play football,
It is more than just a hobby,
It is more than just a game,
It is about teamwork,
Winning matches,
Working together,
Co-operating with each other,
And you have one goal
In your mind
And that's to win the league,
And to win the cup,
To become the best you can be,
To never give up,
Even if it seems impossible,
And that's what football
Is all about to me.

Louis Johnson (12)
Blenheim High School, Epsom

I Have A Dream

I have a dream
To be a scientist,
To make colourful bangs
And to make big explosions.

I have a dream
To be a scientist,
To send rockets into
Dark, wonderful space.

I have a dream.

Charlie Lord (12)
Blenheim High School, Epsom

No More Animal Cruelty!

I have a wish
To end the pain,
To end the cruelty,
Be free again.

I have a hope
To watch them glow,
To leave them be
And let them go.

I have a dream
To kill the bad,
To give the happy
To the sad.

To help the dogs,
To save the cats,
To help the monkeys,
The rabbits, the rats.

Stop the research,
Stop the testing,
Safe at home
They should be resting.

Once again I say, I see,
So once again, let them free!

Amy Seaton (12)
Blenheim High School, Epsom

I Had A Dream

I had a dream about being as rich as Eminem
And to be a millionaire,
Have a massive house like him with a pond
And an indoor and outdoor swimming pool,
Plus my own club and ten kitchens around the house.
In every bedroom, a bathroom with a swimming pool in it.

Grant Worley-Smith (11)
Blenheim High School, Epsom

I Have A Dream . . .

I have an amazing dream that one day
I will become like my sister, Emma.
Her beautiful eyes glisten in the room of darkness,
Her long, wonderful blonde hair flows around with her gracefully,
Her face is so perfect, why can't mine be?

Emma is a kind, caring person,
Always there when you're hurt.
I think she has been sent down from Heaven
To wipe away all the horrible dirt!

My sister makes me happy when I'm sad,
She wipes away all my wet tears.
Now I am very glad,
Because my sister and I love each other,
So we can forget about our terrible fears!

Sarah Hopson (12)
Blenheim High School, Epsom

Life Dreams

Shapes and lines
of all different kinds
can make the world around us.

If you painted the world
the way you wanted it to be,
life could see a whole
different perspective.

Colour and tone
made on this little stone
changes throughout the day.

But if I had a dream
to make you see
life is real,
so let it be.

Emma Woolman (13)
Blenheim High School, Epsom

I Have A Dream For A Cure

If you had the same frustration,
The same jealousy,
But no determination,
You would know how it feels.

I have a dream that one day
My brother and others
Will be free,
Like you and me.

If only it did not hurt as much,
If it could be as soft as a touch,
Life would be so much easier.
Simple, plain and no hurt at all.

The injections and the blood tests,
Without them it would be best.
Children would no longer be jealous,
But would be equal and the same.

So for people with diabetes,
I write you this poem,
Because I have a dream
That you will no longer live with difficulties.

Amy Belcher (13)
Blenheim High School, Epsom

I Have A Dream

I wish my nan was still alive,
I wish she did not die,
I wish she never had cancer,
I wish she was alright,
I wish I could see her,
I always think of her,
I wish she came back,
I will always love her,
I would never let her go.
We all love her.

Ashley Price (12)
Blenheim High School, Epsom

Dreams

All over the world
People love dreams,
Dreams about life,
Dreams without themes.

Some people dream of food,
Some people dream of drink,
Some people curl up in a ball,
Some people just sit and think.

Some people dream on their back,
Some people dream on their side,
Those who live in war
Often crouch down and hide.

As for me, on the other hand,
I dream of a peaceful life,
One without gunshots,
One without a knife.

Jo Kendall (13)
Blenheim High School, Epsom

Hoping For The Future

I have a dream where people have wings
And can see outside their own world,
See beyond the riches and see the poor.
I have a dream where there are no wars between nations,
I have a dream of seeing that day.

Ben McCarthy (13)
Blenheim High School, Epsom

I Have A Dream

I have a dream, it's not impossible,
It's actually the only thing possible.
I would like to be a model one day soon,
Kids looking up to me, shining like the moon.

Everything around me just keeps spinning,
All around me everyone's winning.
I try and work hard, but it gets thrown back in my face,
My mum just says, 'It's not a race.'

All my family helps me non-stop,
I love them all like fizzy pop.
I have a dream, it's not impossible,
It's actually the only thing possible.

Emma Titchener (12)
Blenheim High School, Epsom

Stand Together

If everyone's the same
And no one is to blame,
And if we all stand together,
Then everyone is clever.

Separation is wrong,
So we've got to be strong,
And if we all stand together,
Then everyone is clever.

If there are two lots it's bad,
It makes people sad,
But if we all stand together,
Then everyone is clever.

If everyone's the same
And no one is to blame,
And if we all stand together,
Then everyone is clever.

Lauren Miller (13)
Blenheim High School, Epsom

I Have A Dream

I could know what others were thinking

H elp the ones with disabilities
A pplaud the good things people do
V isit the poor and hungry
E scape terror and hate

A chieve my goals in life

D o something about the world
R elive your happiest moments
E njoy the great times
A nd break down at the bad times
M aking everyone happy.

Chris Childs (13)
Blenheim High School, Epsom

Poverty

The cold is bitter,
The night is dim,
No food in days,
Hunger kicks in.

His stomach rumbles,
He hears his brother cry,
He is worried
That they both may die.

The cardboard box is rotting,
The clothes are getting old,
They cling to each other
As they hide from the cold.

It's damp, it's dark,
It's lonely too,
How would you feel
If this was you?

Jane Osborne (13)
Blenheim High School, Epsom

People

I look up to people
Who in my eyes are perfect.
I know it's not true,
But I think the world is new.

I look up to people
Who help others,
Charity workers
And doctors too.

Someday I dream
To become a teacher
And to be
A professional dancer.

Some people are good,
Some people are bad,
God sorts out the good
And the police sort out the bad.

The world spins around,
When you get dizzy you fall to the ground,
So when I dream to become one of these,
I beg and I plead, please, oh please.

Ellen Frier (11)
Blenheim High School, Epsom

Peace

Peace is a feeling, not just an action,
It is not impossible, it is just not wanted.
Bad people cannot live with it.
Without *peace*, there is war and war causes pain.

If people can work together, *peace* can do its job,
Because when *peace* is around, happiness is created,
And when happiness is around, love is made,
Love, happiness, *peace*, forever!

Stephen Verrell (13)
Blenheim High School, Epsom

My Life Of Fulfilling Dreams

I have a dream
And I would love to become
A gold medallist athlete
And become number one.

I have a dream of
Running, jumping and throwing,
And keep a victory
Going, going and going.

I have a dream of
Winning the cup
Because netball's the sport
That I big up.

I have a dream of
Leaping, spinning and prancing,
Having audiences, having props,
On the stage doing dancing.

I have a dream of
Meeting Carolina Kluft,
Teaching me new skills
So I can become tough.

I have dreams
And I would love them to come true.
I would love to be the person
That everyone knew!

Ellen Rowley (12)
Blenheim High School, Epsom

School Dream

I have a dream . . .

That inside every school
There will be one rule,
Where everything is cool
And no one is a fool.

I have a dream . . .

That homework will be banished
And working will have vanished,
Everything will be fun
Because I'll tell you how things will be run.

I have a dream . . .

That all school dinners will be tasty,
Not gooey slime in pastry,
But chicken, pasta, pizza and cheese,
Well maybe a few veggies like potatoes and peas.

But most of all
I want this dream to come true,
And who's gonna help me?
Him, her and *you!*

Tyler Cook-Abbott (12)
Blenheim High School, Epsom

I Have A Dream Of A Place . . .

I have a dream of a place
That's not perfect, but not imperfect.

I have a dream of a place
That's not peaceful, but not noisy.

I have a dream of a place
That's not colourful, but not dull.

I have a dream of a place
That's not bigger than life, but is not as small as an ant.

I have a dream of a place
That's not fair, but is not dark.

I have a dream of a place
That's not perfect.

James Way (15)
Charters School, Ascot

I Have A Dream

My dream is something with a white ball.
It sounds like a massive roar when it hits the back of the net.
I can feel the wind blow through my hair when I race to get the ball.
Today this is the one, this is the final of the FA Cup.
I walk through the tunnel thinking to myself,
We are going to win the FA Cup.
We run out and there I can see hundreds and thousands of people.
FA Cup final is coming to the end, we are 1-0 up,
Then I hear the final whistle go
And we have won the FA Cup!

Harry Hammonds (15)
Charters School, Ascot

I Have A Dream . . .

I wish that I could mess with time
And think before I speak,
Then I would never regret
A single sentence of my life.
Hateful eyes would look beyond
My dreaded mouth of words,
And I wouldn't have to sweep up
The fragments of someone's heart.
People would see me
For who I want to be,
And sleepless nights would crush someone else.
If only I knew where the dice would roll
So that I could learn the script
And I would never suffer the consequences.
If only I, the tiny seed,
Could grow to the size of a castle.

Natalie Jones (12)
Charters School, Ascot

?

I am swimming through sea air,
I am the cold wind biting me on the cheek,
My eyes aspire to be a rainbow,
I have ears that come in the shape of musical notes,
I am clothes that wear themselves,
I am the walls speaking their mind,
I am my arms spinning right round to 3 o'clock,
My hair can be cotton soft,
My brain is a 4D baby girl,
Green is my body.
Who am I?

I am my own dreams.

Gemma Tunbridge (15)
Charters School, Ascot

I Have A Dream . . .

That greed would go away by the kiss of the moonlight.
I have a dream
That the boat of selfishness would drown in the ocean of life.
I have a dream
That death would only be after evil.
I have a dream
That illness is money, here today, gone tomorrow.
I have a dream
That anger is the swallows that emigrate.
I have a dream
That betrayal is the infinitesimal ants we squish.
I have a dream
That temptation is only a mirage.
I have a dream
That ignorance is a burning candle.
I have a dream
That the vortex of fear would stop spinning horror.
I have a dream,
A wish,
A hope,
That happiness is your spirit, let it be with you . . .

Zahra Rajabalipour (14)
Charters School, Ascot

I Have A Dream

My dream would sound like the flash of a camera,
My dream would feel like a fluffy pillow,
My dream would sound like a ball hitting the ground,
The first visual image I see is of Wimbledon.
In my perfect world there are no suffering people,
In my perfect world there is no poverty,
In my perfect world there is no hunger.

Cara Gilham (14)
Charters School, Ascot

I Have A Dream

I have a dream,
It merges
Questions and
Fraternises with my emotions,
Knocking down the wall
Between fact and reality,
Tempting me with subtle curiosity,
Driving me further into the deep abyss,
Answering my screams
With futile replies,
Presenting me with spectres
Of empty promises
And twisted reminders
Of my buried lie,
Keeping in the wake of my imagination,
Ready to pounce on my hopelessness,
Manifest and feed on my pain
With heartless pity or just self-indulgence.

Jessica Smith (13)
Charters School, Ascot

Football

My dream is about a ball,
The roaring cheer of fans.
As I score, I hear the sound,
The sound when the ball
Hits the back of the net.
The teamwork of my players.
We are the World Cup winners!

Billy Campin (14)
Charters School, Ascot

I Have A Dream

I have a dream
To make you people see
That I'm the best rugby player
You've ever seen.

Throughout the game
Everyone's chanting my name,
They shout out loud and clear,
'You're the best rugby player
We've seen in years!'

It was a scrum,
But the ref's so dumb
That he gave it to the other team,
Then the fly half ran off with speed.
I took him down,
He fell to the ground
With a loud thud,
Had a bleeding mouth.

At the end of the game
We shook hands and said, 'Well played.'
I got man of the match,
And that was that.

Shaun Spencer (12)
Charters School, Ascot

I Have A Dream

The beautiful melding of brown and green,
The gush and rush of pouring cream,
The flying and crashing of breaking rain,
Today and now there is no such thing,
But I believe that someday there will be
The English version of pistachio ice cream.

George Winstone (14)
Charters School, Ascot

I Have A Dream

I have a dream, a vision,
A thought.
I have a dream that only I can see.

I have a dream
In the day,
Plus at night.
I have a dream, a vision,
A thought.

I have dreams,
They are good,
They are bad,
Many dreams I have had.

I have a dream,
They take me away to a remote place,
They take me to a quiet place,
A quiet place where I can escape.

I have a dream, a vision,
A thought.
I have a dream that only I can see.

Michael Guard (15)
Charters School, Ascot

Dream

I turned around and saw a sky of orange.
Screeching of monkeys fill the surroundings,
The floor starts to move like a plate of jelly,
Today I am in an unusual land,
I am squelching through mud,
Mud that is organically green.

Adam Clarke (15)
Charters School, Ascot

Sweet Bonanza

Imagine:

Hearing
The crunchy almond thins snapping and popping below your feet,
The green Smartie grass rustles,
The Galaxy chocolate tree trunks crack and snap, harvested to eat,
The M & M bluebirds rustling their edible feathers,
The children crying and shrieking with laughter, playing with their
                                                                                    fruit pastille frisbies.

Seeing
The houses with gingerbread roofs just out of the oven and never
                                                                                    running out of flavour,
The Mars bar police cars driving around to make sure the sweet
                                                                                    world is safe,
People swimming in honey swimming pools.

Touching
The sticky toffee golden river,
The red lollipop parasols, yum, delicious,
The melting chocolate Aero fountain,
The Jelly Tots raindrops.

Eating
The Galaxy wood chairs in your house,
A stilts-man Twirl's stilts,
White and dark chocolate canoes on the caramel river.

I had a lovely dream.

Luke Webbe (11)
Charters School, Ascot

I Have A Dream

Pollution and cars,
Criminals and guns,
Dangerous streets,
Children knocked down.

Golden, crisp flowers,
Silver-lined clouds,
Mint green grass,
Children found playing.

Extinction and cruelty,
Poaching and stealth,
Trees cut down,
Terrorism lurks near.

Fresh species arrive,
Protection is in action,
Peace is created,
Blossom trees swaying.

Poverty and death,
Starvation and disease,
Money is tight,
Orphans left homeless.

Newborn babies,
Food to spare,
Who needs money
When everyone's together?

Gwen McNamara-Sena (14)
Charters School, Ascot

I Have A Dream

My dream is to play piano to the best of my ability,
The sound is a piano playing constantly,
The texture would be like silk, the way the keys feel.
All you could hear is a light breeze
In the background from the piano.
The usual image is of piano keys playing.

In my perfect world, there are no distractions
From everyone being happy.

Today I got closer to achieving my dream.
I will achieve my dream one day in the future.
Future, for me, will hopefully be soon.

Lucy Wigmore (14)
Charters School, Ascot

Fly Around The World

Up so high, flying over the big blue oceans,
The engine of the plane roaring through the sky,
The plane racing through the sky.
Today my journey takes me to Australia.

I see the Sydney Opera House in the distance,
Australia today, Japan tomorrow.
Landing in Tokyo, the land of gadgets,
Landing in America, the land of films.

Going round all the states
Seeing all the sights,
Flying back to Europe,
Soaking up the sun.

Marc Lowdon (14)
Charters School, Ascot

I Have A Dream

Imagine
Hearing the voice of angels singing,
My wings in the breeze,
Laughing of people, all ages,
Smelling the floral smell of fresh roses,
Touching the wind
That gets caught up in my hair,
Soft, sheep-like clouds,
A hand as gentle as a kiss,
As I turn around,
Seeing a crowd of people
With faces carved by angels
Who are happy and laughing,
An old friend that grabs my hand,
A friend and the best teacher in the world,
I start to feel sadness
When a hand punches my heart,
I am in Heaven
And remember it's only a dream,
Tears pour out of my eyes.

Jenna Grant (12)
Charters School, Ascot

I Have A Dream

I dream that I will be wealthy,
My wallet is packed full of new, crispy green notes.
The jingle of the coins in my pocket,
The coins rubbing against each other.
Today I will dream my dream again.
I dream my dream each and every night.
Night is what I look forward to,
For at night I dream my dream of wealth.

Jack Walsh (14)
Charters School, Ascot

I Had A Dream Too!

Martin had a dream of a
White boy and a little black girl getting along,
And dreamt that no one did wrong.

He had a dream that we all cared for people,
No matter who or what they are,
And his dream has made a difference
And affected people from afar.

I had a dream something like his the other night.
I dreamt no one would ever argue or fight.
Over the colour of our skin,
And whether some are fat and some thin.

Everyone becomes a different person,
Everyone's unique.
Some tall or small, some strong, some weak.

We have to start accepting more people for who they are.
Some people wish on their lucky star
That they won't get criticised ever again
And bullies won't put them through that pain.

So if you have had a dream like Martin's or mine,
Stick to what you have dreamt
And you will fit in the world just fine!

Katie Neck (14)
Charters School, Ascot

I Had A Dream

I had a dream
That I could go to the park
Without feeling scared and alone,
That kids didn't laugh because I was different,
That people weren't afraid to be my friend,
That I wasn't ashamed to look at myself in the mirror.
But now I am awake
And I know this is only a dream.

Jasmine Smith (12)
Charters School, Ascot

A Ferrari

My dream is a sparkly red car which goes fast.
My car can be heard from the engine of the car going *brum, brum*.
The Ferrari that I drive goes very fast along the ground.
Today I woke up and jumped into my new flashy car.
I got onto the road and had a spin around in my car.
Cars are the coolest things in the entire universe.
This would be the greatest, to think that it could happen to me.
I would speed around the area I live and have a great time.
My dream is a sparkly red car which goes fast.

Alexander O'Mahony (15)
Charters School, Ascot

I Have A Dream

I have a dream
In the land of chocolate
Where it rains Maltesers
And the rivers flow with white chocolate.
The crunch of liquorice under my feet
And the roads of icing ready to lick,
The fountain of chocolate
In the town square
And the ice cream hills
Behind the Smarties rainbow.
I have a dream,
A most wonderful dream.

Aled Griffith-Swain (12)
Charters School, Ascot

I Have A Dream . . .

A dream that I could have a holiday of a lifetime
Sitting by a romantic sunset on the beach,
Swimming with swift dolphins
That dip elegantly in the clear blue sea.
Ice-skating in a moonlit city with passion,
Being in London in 2012.

If this dream were to be true,
Then I would fly on an aeroplane
And stay in a luxurious hotel,
Watching the long shadows of the pyramids grow.
I can only dream about digging in the beautiful Valley of the Kings
And visiting the twisting mile on an undulating camel.

Dreaming of living a life in a less populated area
Is everything I've ever wanted,
But to go there would be better than imagining.

Daniel Mucklow (12)
Charters School, Ascot

I Have A Dream

That life was as long as you wished it to be,
That everyone had food
And no one died of drought.
There were no flames of hatred
To anyone or anything
And global warming a thing of the past.
But these things are only a dream
And life must go on
And humanity must make its mistakes.

Anton Lindley-DeCaire (12)
Charters School, Ascot

A Short Dream

At night I dream like any other person,
The usual stuff, Spain, giraffes,
The ability to sing,
But there's one particular thing,
To not be so short,
Because being short brings difficulties into life.
I get terrible neck pains, you see,
From having to crane my neck
To look people in the eye,
And when I go to look in the mirror,
I have to jump.
Just little things, like being in a crowd,
Make me blind.
Sometimes I do wish for the difficulties to cease,
So why can't my dream come true?
Why can't I be tall?

Helena Winstone (11)
Charters School, Ascot

I Have A Dream

I have a dream,
I have it every night,
My dream is simple.
I dream I am here in this war,
But I cannot leave
Because my gun is my soulmate
And my fellow soldiers are my family
And these trenches I sit in are my home.
As I hear the rapid fire deafen me
I realise my dream is simple,
I want to go home!

Jonathan Rotter (13)
Charters School, Ascot

I Have A Dream

I have a dream
That I could go into every shop
And everything I would want would be free!
I go into Schuh and buy all their sassy high heels
And their vintage dolly shoes,
Not forgetting their burning, bright pink Converse.
Next is New Look, buying all their wow factor tops
And flashy mini skirts, also their stripey fashion shorts.
I go into Faith and buy all their bright, sparkly blue pumps
And their hot, pointy high heels and their cute, glistening,
                                                    sequin shoes.
I go into Topshop and buy all their tight, skinny jeans and
                                                    hot chick tops,
But then it all gets too exciting,
I realise it's just a dream.

Esther Whiting (13)
Charters School, Ascot

World Peace

I have a dream that the sky is pink,
The leaves are yellow, the grass is orange.
I have a dream that people
Are calm, pleasant and honest.
I have a dream that the buildings are blue,
The roads are green and the sea is purple.
I have a dream that schools are filled with rainbows,
Amusements are free, animals are safe.
I have a dream that the world is a
Better, brighter place. World peace.

Eleanor Ashton (13)
Charters School, Ascot

I Have A Dream

I have a dream that other children get an education like us
and have as many opportunities as we do.

I have a dream that poverty will end in all countries
and nobody will have to starve to death.

I have a dream that cruelty to children will discontinue
and people will try to do more to help.

I have a dream that money doesn't exist
and everything is free.

I have a dream that all crime will come to an end
and people will see sense.

I have a dream that everyone could be happy in the world
and have no worries.

I have a dream that all my dreams come true
and the world will be perfect.

Reme Sumal (13)
Charters School, Ascot

I Have A Dream

I have a dream to end world hunger,
I have a dream to end all poverty,
I have a dream to end all crime,
I have a dream to end gun violence,
I have a dream for a better world,
I have a dream for world peace,
I have a dream, we all do,
But are they just dreams?
Will they be fulfilled?

Louise Bowers (15)
Charters School, Ascot

I Have A Dream

The poverty,
The attacks,
The dangers,
I have this dream.

The Africans,
The Londoners,
The Americans,
I have this dream.

The children are starving,
There's nothing to eat,
There's nothing to drink,
The water is brown.
I hate this dream.

The London Underground is frightening,
A little object, so many dead.
Five big bangs
And it may happen again.
I hate this dream.

9/11 was ever so scary,
Two skyscrapers,
There's nothing now.
Under the rubble there are lots of good souls.
I hate this dream.

Elliott Woodham (12)
Charters School, Ascot

Teenage Life

There is a part of me
That seems different,
Something I can't see,
Something I can't quite feel,
Something I want to disbelieve,
But I know it's there,
Something that won't disappear.
I have a dream that feeling would fade away,
A thing with others I won't share.
I urge the thought to leave me forever,
The thoughts of
Your past, the boys, make-up and clothes,
You try to get on with your life
But then the haunting feeling reappears
And once again I feel cold and lost.
People in this world feel like this,
People in this world get trapped.
I dream for the world to be made of chocolate,
I also wish for there to be no poverty
And I wish for people to be more open,
Get what you feel inside, out worldwide,
But hold on one minute, this is only a dream,
Let's snap back to reality.

Alexandra Brown (13)
Charters School, Ascot

Cold End

I have a dream,
A dream of now.
To stop this constant
Bickering between
Kennedy and Khrushchev.
Let me sleep in peace,
Without the threat of bombs.
Not to wake up to a world
That has disappeared.
Technology not wasted
On nukes and space.
Who wants to go to the moon?
Who cares?
Think of the starving,
They could do with the money.
Kennedy and Khrushchev
Terrorising the world.
Don't they remember Hiroshima?
Do they want World War III?
'Kennedy has announced he is
Putting a naval blockade on Cuba'
The radio booms.
Peace. That's my dream.
My dream of '62.

Melinda Kerrison (16)
Charters School, Ascot

I Have A Dream

I have a dream of peace and harmony,
Dreams that seem so far away,
The dreams that matter are ignored,
End to poverty, hunger, homelessness,
Dreams that people long to come true.

People get their dreams sometimes,
The dreams of more money and things they don't need.
Dreams I have aren't about all that,
I dream for world peace, not pleasure for me,
So why do those other dreamers get what they want?

I lie at night, my head full of thought,
Thoughts of dreams and hopes for the future,
The dream of peace and harmony,
The dreams that seem so far away.

Beth England (11)
Charters School, Ascot

I Have A Dream . . .

A dream of sweets,
Where the clouds are made of candyfloss
And the grass is made of liquorice.

The shiny, colourful wrappers
With the chewy, tasty, tangy flavours inside
Melting, fizzing and bubbling
On my tongue.

Maltesers, chocolate, bubblegum,
Sherbet, lollipops and jelly babies all around me.
Then I awake.
I had a dream.

Luke Thompson (12)
Charters School, Ascot

I Have A Dream

The earth crumbles beneath my feet, yet the ground stays solid.
Wars, fighting, guns and bombs, is this the life we lead?
Such a shock with London bombings, yet, a normality in Iraq.
To give a little food to people instead of bins
Would not go unnoticed in Third World countries.
We wake up on mattresses placed upon frames,
Less fortunate souls wake with dirt and dust or do not wake at all.
Countries where AIDS is found round every corner,
Countries where children miss school because of a sore throat.
Taps with running water in every home,
Yet in some towns it is a luxury for a pump a mile away.
Why is it so hard for the world to get along?
It could be a lovely place:
No murder, no war, no vandalism or hatred,
Hunger is a distant memory.
The earth *could* be solid beneath my feet, that is my dream.

Caragh Cheesman (11)
Charters School, Ascot

Sweet Dream

I have a dream that the rivers were made from
Smooth, creamy Galaxy,
Haribo would hang tightly on
The colourful, fruity bushes,
Aero lay across every building like brick on brick,
Vividly candyfloss floats across the hot shining sky,
Everlasting popcorn flies out of the hot caramel volcano,
It snows a rainbow of Solero ice cream,
Maltesers roll down the bright green hill,
Lollies bellow out the garden as I peek over the fence
Grabbing onto the pole!
Hot chocolate running down my veins craving for more,
Until the day comes when I can't have what I want,
And I'm in a fairy-tale dream, waiting to wake up,
Hoping not to be ill!

Sara Chouki (12)
Charters School, Ascot

Mr Gogarty

Ten years I've been here with him,
One year till I can leave.
A tragic death to begin this chapter,
That no one can believe.

The death of my headmaster,
He was the perfect guy.
In his pocket was a bright blue hanky,
That matched with his tie.

On the day of our big game,
He'd be cheering from the side,
Getting rather involved with things . . .
'Come on St John's, take pride.'

But all he tried to do
Was to help and do things well.
The end was unbearably sudden,
Like a fun lesson's bell.

We all had respect for him,
Respect that will never die.
The respect for a man we all loved,
Our headmaster, the perfect guy.

Alex Pindar (13)
St John's Beaumont School, Old Windsor

Mr Gogarty

His name was Mr Gogarty
Headmaster of our school SJB
He was the greatest man
Who would always understand
The boys who went to his school.

He would always have his head held high
Whenever he would pass you by
And greet you with, 'Good morning', or 'Good afternoon'.

He would always want to listen to us boys
Yet shouted if ever we made too much noise
But was happy if we looked good.

He would always look smart
Happy if we looked the part
And congratulated us on everything we did right.

At the end of the year
When our work was all done
He would get someone special
To give us the prizes we had won.

Then he would make a great speech
And like a high priest
Preach to our parents the
Good things we did in the past year.

All the old boys from last year
Had to shed a small tear
For they are leaving not to come back
But on the inside the feelings they can't hide
Of the happiness and sadness all mixed
Feeling like a small child of seven, or maybe six.

But now he has left us
The whole school sad because
He has left and will never come back
For we all loved Mr Gogarty
Because of the love he had for the ones
Who went to his and our great school, SJB.

Yet his memory lives on
Long after we have gone
This poem now told you see
And it's for the memory of Mr Gogarty.

Charlie McDermott (13)
St John's Beaumont School, Old Windsor

I Have A Dream

I have a dream . . .
That I could have the courage of Muhammad Ali,
That I could be famous and a hero like him,
That I could be a great example and figure like him,
That I could fight as well as him,
That I could inspire people like he does,
That I could have such a good talent as he does,
That I could have the determination he does,
That I could be a legend like him,
That I could be so well known like him,
That I could have the power and importance he does,
That I could amaze people with a talent like he has,
That I could be as athletic as him,
That I will be known when I'm dead, like he will be,
That I could be as strong as him.
I wish I could box like Muhammad Ali in every single way.

Dominic Bhamber (13)
St John's Beaumont School, Old Windsor

Winston Churchill

I left my school for Sandhurst
When I was only a teen
And as I left, I turned eighteen.
I left the army in 1899
And after that had nothing to decline.

I then became an MP, a conservative whatnot.
This all changed when Henry Campbell was shot.
On the war outbreak of 1914 I joined the council of war,
And this spelt danger, of that I was sure.

I then rejoined the conservatives with at all administration,
When I would later become head of the whole organisation.
War broke out and I was a lord,
This mean I surely wasn't bored.

Adolf Hitler came in 1933
And Mr Chamberlain could not all see.
He resigned to me in 1940
And I set out to get that little shorty.

I led the people through thick and thin
And didn't dump one in the bin.
We fought them on the beaches,
We fought them in the sky,
And never once I told a lie.

Toby Tanner (13)
St John's Beaumont School, Old Windsor

My Deep Fire

The motivating beat starts
A thousand suns glow again
The deep fire burns within
My soul cries out
My prosperity earns its being

A want, a need, a dream

My being striving for something
Something too deep for words
A passion revealed through my body
Dedicated to the creator of my talent
My shield, my strength
I move with grace
The bass blinds me
In a trance
My light laughs at its shadows
The purifying force of my heart
Dance is the air I breathe
The unbroken beat
My wild heartbeat
My unstoppable feet.

Christina Maria Ciara Darmanin (17)
St Mary's School, Ascot

I Have A Dream . . .

I have a dream . . .
I want to be a football player for Manchester United

I dream of shooting a ball into the goal
I see myself skidding on the ground, doing a handstand,
doing a roly-poly and jumping over the fence to the crowd,
I rip my shirt off and chuck it at the crowd.

Paul Bird (12)
The Avenue School, Reading

Princess

I wish I were a princess.
I wonder if it'd be like the cartoons and fantasy films.
I'd have white dresses, blue dresses and pink dresses,
just like bridesmaids.
My mum and dad would be a queen and king,
my brother a famous prince, my sisters, evil princesses!
I would be very spoilt and wish that the rainbow would stay
over my palace all the time.
My white bed would be enveloped by rich drapes hanging
on both sides.
I'd have a pony with its own cosy home, fresh green grass
that would melt in his mouth, a nice bushy tail and plaits in his hair.
He'd be called Snowflake.
I'd ride my pony until a handsome Prince Charming came for me.
He would propose to me and become a lovely husband.
His pony, Snowy, would fall in love with my Snowflake.

Skye Gardner (14)
The Avenue School, Reading

My Dream

If I were a famous singer
I could go to different places like India
I would meet loads of people
I would be popular like 50 Cent
I would have experience of the outside world
I could see lots of girls
I would be going on TV programmes, like GMTV
I would be making CDs for people
I could travel around the world
I would get loads of money
I could get a big house at the seaside.

Shane Donnell (14)
The Avenue School, Reading

My Dreams

My dream is that every disabled child/adult is given the correct wheelchair for their needs.

The reason for this dream is because I am struggling to get the correct wheelchair for me, the reason this is so important is that some people need comfort; some people, like myself, need a light, well-balanced wheelchair for everyday life because I am, what is called, an 'active user' which means I can move myself about and I can back-wheel balance; that means I can sit on my back wheels and get up kerbs.

Ben McGifford (12)
The Avenue School, Reading

My Dream

I have a dream to swim with dolphins
because I like their fins
and how they come up from the water
and splash people.

I have a dream to go to Hawaii
because I want to dance to the beat
of Hula-hula.

I have a dream to take my nan out
for a posh meal because she deserves it.

Antony Thomas (15)
The Avenue School, Reading

I Have A Dream . . .

I have a dream that I will become a wrestler
and get chosen in the draft lottery draw.
I'll go to the Raw Arena and face the WWE champion.
When I'm the WWE champion,
I will buy a nice flat and carry on with my job.

Spencer Jarman (12)
The Avenue School, Reading

My Dream

I wish that I were the Prime Minister.
I would get to rule the country.
I would help the poor people.
I'd give every child pocket money every week.
I would also take no taxes from old people.
I would also help schools.
I would build a giant computer room.
I would also help people by putting more police on the streets
                                        to stop robbers.
I would try my hardest to stop wars.
I would also create more jobs.

Christopher Sarney (14)
The Avenue School, Reading

My Dream

In my dream I am a pirate.
I can go to sea in my boat.
I will sail towards my castle.
I will wear a pirate hat and a patch over my eye.
My parrot called Tiger will sit on my shoulder.
I'll have a knife and some big boots.
One of my legs will be wooden.
One day I'll have a fight with another pirate,
but we'll make up and be friends again,
this is because I'll be a kind pirate.

Gulhasib Akhter (13)
The Avenue School, Reading

I Have A Dream

I have a dream about being a nurse,
so I could treat the sick people.
I would like them all to get better.

Emma King (12)
The Avenue School, Reading

My Dream

I wish
I could fly to the moon
I would smell it
and take a bite from it
to find out if it really
is cheese.
I would make a camp
on the lumpy surface.
I would light a fire
and cook some cheesy
moon on toast.
I would lie down and sniff
the delicious aroma all night long.
In the morning I'd come back home
and tell everyone that the moon
really is cheese.
I'd ask Jamie Oliver to make
me a giant burger and bun,
then I would have the world's biggest cheeseburger
with a squashed moon cheese slice.

Luke Lewendon (15)
The Avenue School, Reading

Going For Gold

My greatest dream
Is that one day
I will become an Olympic athlete.
I dream of winning lots of gold medals.
I will be famous.
I will be a good role model.
I will meet interesting people.
I will try to train every day.
I will run in the world's biggest stadiums.
I will get fit every day.
I would like to swim in the Olympics.

Matthew Lewendon (15)
The Avenue School, Reading

My Dream

My dream would be, to be a famous chef like Jamie Oliver.
I would have my own TV show on BBC1 and Ainsley Harriet
would wash up all the dishes.

I would travel to lots of different countries and try every type of food,
and if they were poor and didn't have any food, I would make them
a giant sausage roll, 100 feet long!

By the time I'm 20, I will cook the best chicken curry in India,
the best pizza in Italy and the best roast dinner in England!

I'll have restaurants all over the world and people will come from
miles around to try 'Lee's famous hotpot'!

Lee Perrett (13)
The Avenue School, Reading

My Dreams

In my dreams I am a charity worker for my church.
I am in Mozambique helping people.
I would help the orphans,
I would build them a place to stay, with a big park.
I would bring pens, paper and books and build them a school,
so they could learn everything that we learn.
It would be a nice environment,
full of fun things to do.
I would clear all the rubbish away
so it would be somewhere they would feel loved and safe.
I would build a giant kitchen,
that would never run out of food for them,
so they would never go hungry again.

Sophie Drake (14)
The Avenue School, Reading

I Have A Dream

I have a dream that we will be equal,
I have a dream that we will all do right,
'I have a dream,' says Martin Luther King.
We all have a dream we hope will come true,
We all have a dream we want to achieve,
We all have a dream that will hopefully happen.
Poverty should stop now in Africa,
Murderers should get their lives snatched away,
Animal testing is wrong, stop it now.
Some may have small dreams, some may have big dreams,
Some may not come true, some may be achieved,
But everyone has that special wish.
The dreams are as big as huge lions,
They may be as small as a squeaky mouse,
They are your dreams, they are your whole future.
They are like sparkling stars in the night sky
You need to watch them and what they're doing.
Martin Luther King achieved good by this,
His speech changed people's lives for the better,
He did what he wanted in his great life.
So if you want your life dream to happen,
Don't sit there and wait like a dead man,
Get up and say, 'I do have a dream!'

Helen Gardner (13)
The Downs School, Newbury

Care For Hair

I have a dream that I must just share,
Where people are not judged by the colour of their hair,
I don't care for the way you look and stare,
Only because there is a shade of ginger in the air.
You need to open your hearts and open your eyes
And see that really we are quite nice guys.

Luke Griffiths (16)
The Downs School, Newbury

I Have A Dream

Carbon monoxide gets blown out from cars,
creating yet another cloud of pollution,
collecting above the grassy apple's surface.

Acid rain falls from the heavens above,
it falls as fast as a bullet train speeds,
the bullet train carrying our vitamins A, B and C.

But when we take a bite into our fruit,
a diesel taste explores our mouth,
instead of a sweet and juicy fruit taste.

When one too many cars have been made,
where will our Earth stand?
We all fear the worst.

A world without cars, is a girl without her best friend,
although one day, these monoxide monsters,
will be destroyed.

But if we put all our dreams together,
we can find a key for a new beginning,
a key to a door, leaving all our problems behind.

The ozone layer fixed,
modern technology gone,
maybe this world could be so different.

Just use your dream to get somewhere,
do something about this,
just use your mind,
create your dream.

Alice Malthouse (13)
The Downs School, Newbury

A High Price To Pay

In her Armani suit, she looked sleek
The picture of modern-day chic
Totally cool with her Gucci handbag
Until she reached in and pulled out a fag.

Why spray with Prada scent every day
If you're going to smell like a dirty ashtray?
Her possessions may have been expensive
But the damage smoke caused was extensive.

She had less and less friends by the day
Passive smoking drove them all away
The men in her life wouldn't kiss
They would rather just give it a miss.

While drinking in a trendy wine bar
She had the most embarrassing moment so far
When told that if she wanted to smoke
She should go out - leave her Bacardi and Coke.

When diagnosed with a fatal lung tumour
She lost her entire sense of humour
With hindsight, the price that she paid
Far too high - now her life was to fade.

Her children were both very brave
When they lowered her into her grave
'Taken too soon' her posh headstone read
If she had quit she wouldn't be dead!

Nicole Rumble (14)
The Downs School, Newbury

I Have A Dream

I have a dream,
When there's always an open door,
When the world is a team,
There is no war,
I can make a difference,
And so can you.

I have a dream,
When pollution stops,
All rivers are clean,
And poverty drops,
If I can do it,
So can you.

I have a dream,
Of love and soul,
Every face has a shining beam,
No heart as black as coal,
I can see a future,
Where all my dreams come true.

Camilla Chichester (12)
The Downs School, Newbury

I Have A Dream

I have a dream that people will stop hating each other.
I have a dream that world hunger will end.
I have a dream that there is world peace.
I have a dream that money won't take over the world.
I have a dream that pollution will end.
I have a dream that sickness will end.
I have a dream that people will be equal.
I have a dream people will respect me for who I am.
I have a dream that everyone will have this dream.

Courtney Holmes (12)
The Downs School, Newbury

I Have A Dream

Into the sunlight,
Out of the shadows,
That's how the world should be,
Not a dark hole.

The world never stops spinning,
Because that's up to us.

It takes courage to stand up for what's right.
But people do it.

The world is still here today because of us,
And the world can be gone because of us as well.

Our job is to take care of the world,
Not to destroy it.

We have dreams,
Others have nightmares,
Every day is a nightmare for them.

We dream today,
For others tomorrow.

Matt Northfield (12)
The Downs School, Newbury

The Perfect World

The perfect world to me would be a world without poverty.
A world where there is no crime and everyone can feel safe.
A world where every country gets along and there's peace
                                        and no war.
A world where animals and people can live in perfect harmony.
A world where people can learn to be friends and not fight.
A world where no one goes without
And everyone gets what they need, not just what they want.

That's my perfect world.

Charley New (13)
The Downs School, Newbury

I Have A Dream

A famished child
Pain in her eyes
Begging for food
Alone and tired

A homeless man
Hiding his face
His hands outstretched
Lonely and cold

A weak woman
Reaping the fields
Her hands aching
Dying inside

No more famine
Inequity
Destitution
This is my dream.

Joni Richardson (13)
The Downs School, Newbury

I Have A Dream

Dreams begin as a single strand of silk
They can grow into elaborate webs,
Or be crushed by the shadow of despair.

Dreams begin small, like a seed in the ground.
Slowly it blossoms and grows scarlet petals;
Slowly it blossoms and grows jagged thorns.

Believing in dreams, will make them come true.
However unlikely, a strand can be woven,
A seed can blossom and a hope can flourish.

Emilia Ramirez (13)
The Downs School, Newbury

I Have A Dream! The Future

I have a dream, when poverty is gone,
Children in Africa released from hunger
Hunger replaced with schools and health care
Africa, prosperous like a blooming flower
Shooting up through the ground towards the future.

I have a dream where peace spreads throughout the land
Violence fading like colour in the sunshine
Weapons destroyed like the job they were supposed to do,
Women and children equal to man
Respect welcomed back like an old friend

I have a dream where climate change is halted,
Like a car stopping suddenly,
The trees are reborn, reclaiming the land
The air is as pure as a glass of pure water
Cars that harm nobody

I have a dream when people can be happy,
No need to worry about work and school
Attention to health, no need for wealth.

David Seymour (13)
The Downs School, Newbury

Marine Biology

Waking up to Africa
The birds ringing in my ears
I have a dream
To dive to the bottom of the sea
Swim with the dolphins
Wrestle with the seaweed
Find out about the bottom of the sea
Which creature is the biggest, boldest
The smallest, shyest of them all
Marine biology is my future
I have a dream . . .

Charlotte MacRae (12)
The Downs School, Newbury

I Have A Dream

There once was a strong and powerful chain
Which linked the races throughout the luscious land
But through time this chain did wither and wear
Being pulled on either side by the races

And as time went on the pressure grew stronger
Eating away at the once muscular chain
They looked down on each other like they were dogs
Forgetting that once they were all the same

As the pressure rose, the government was
Torn apart like paper, leaving only chaos
The scraps produced a flame of corruption
The fire was torn at the centre of the chain

As the inferno blazed on like an angry bull
The chain weakened with the immense heat
The land all around was a battlefield
Habitable by none, it was not safe

As races split the country divided
Torn apart by its own racial abuse
What was once a flourishing paradise
Was now just a barren battlefield

After these years, the chain was on its last legs
Withering with governmental corruption
And the determined races on either side
It was nearing the end of this scorn and hate

Finally one day the chain did break
Like a thousand bombs exploding with menace
Everything was ruined, neither side won
The country was destroyed by a shockwave of scorn.

Tom Wigg (13)
The Downs School, Newbury

I Have A Dream

I have a dream that the world could be clean,
Clear of rubbish and no scraps to be seen.
There would be no air pollution at all,
The air temperature would not rise or fall.

Every person would have somewhere to go,
Everyone would have a home of their own.
The perfect world is way too much to ask,
The world would find that too much of a task.

I have a dream that the world could be right,
Free of war, free of battle, free of fights.
So many people get injured and killed,
With guns and weapons the world is then filled.

Families get torn apart, people taken,
Left to sleep they'll never awaken.
Some people kill for revenge, maybe gain,
They cause destruction and a lot of pain.

I have a dream that we will climb those stairs,
Stairs up to Heaven, they're right and fair.
One step at a time and we'll reach the top,
All the wars, fighting and battles will stop.

But what about all those childhood dreams?
Pink horses and robots with laser beams.
What will be done about those fantasies?
Stored and forgotten, never to be seen.

They're happy and bright with nothing bad,
But in reality our lives are sad.
Why can't we live in those pink, fluffy worlds?
The ones that are dreamt by young little girls.

Instead we live in a world full of sin,
If only we could climb up those stairs.

Emma Daniel (12)
The Downs School, Newbury

I Have A Dream

Walking through an endless maze of disappointment and regret
No way out, not even a short cut, nothing but darkness.
Every day feels like a lifetime, plenty of time
For something to go wrong.

I have a dream that one day I will be let out of my prison cell,
Released into the real world, allowing myself to be me
And not someone who I hate.

Twists and turns of rights and wrongs,
Nothing happening smoothly,
Falling, stumbling and tripping over continuous amounts of obstacles
Through my maze of hatred.

I have a dream that there will be peace,
And a world filled with happiness,
Not a world filled with regret and sadness.

There should be a light, glowing inside me,
Waiting for something good to happen,
But that light will soon fade out and soon become dark
As there is nothing for me to be proud of,
Nothing for me to be happy about, nothing for me to smile for.

I have a dream that I will be proud and happy with myself
For everything I have achieved.
I'll walk through that door with a smile on my face,
Telling myself I'm amazing.

Slowly the maze will come to an end,
But until then I keep on walking
Through the muddy path of sadness,
Until my light begins to shine.

Libby Hordos (13)
The Downs School, Newbury

I Have A Dream - Every Day, Every Week

I have a dream every day, every week,
That everyone believes we're all equal
And nobody prejudiced for their skin.

I have a dream every day, every week,
That those who die will be justified,
Male, female, young, old, black, coloured or white.

I have a dream every day, every week,
Of Earth where chess game nations are extinct,
And where the chess pieces are like the board

I have a dream every day, every week,
Where racist words are completely obsolete,
And everyone sees violence can't bring peace.

I have a dream every day, every week,
Where people in airports are never stopped,
Cos terrorism and bombs are all gone.

I have a dream every day, every week,
Where policing is just a part-time job,
And armies fight, purely with their words.

But this is where I wake and my dream ends
My mind snaps back into reality,
Cos none of this will ever, ever happen,
Cos while there are humans, conflict never goes,
But still, while I have this dream and I sleep,
My heart and soul smile happily with my face,
As I imagine an equal world of peace.

Chris Abbott (13)
The Downs School, Newbury

I Have A Dream

In my dream, there is a white wall, pure, fresh
There is innocence, perfection and faith
Then there is paint splattered over my wall
First it is red, I feel raged with anger!
Then orange, I'm filled with desire, pleasure
Soon there is yellow; I'm calm, happy, fresh
Green, envy, like a madman for sanity
Blue, my wisdom is tested by loyalty
Purple, I'm superior, I want more money
I can do anything, the world is in my palm
Lastly, black, the elegance of evil

I step back to look at my wall, once pure
There is no white to be seen, I wake up

The wall is still there, standing tall, reality.

But then pleasure without lust, without greed
And love without hate with purity and faith
Can only lead to happiness, my *dream!*

Ashleigh Evans (13)
The Downs School, Newbury

A Dream For Success

Take your dream from your thoughts
And stir in some success.
Mix in a generous amount of hope and time,
There will be a few errors,
But you will sort it out by what comes to mind,
Now this may take a few months
Or even a year or two.
If you follow and care about your dream
And don't give up,
You'll reach your goal!

Joe Davies (13)
The Downs School, Newbury

I Have A Dream

I have a dream, a wonderful dream.
A mysterious, sparkling walkway surrounds,
Glistening crystals creak beneath my bare feet.
Curiously gliding through,
Through the ice-covered mystery around me

Leading to a twinkling silver jewel,
Engulfed in a giant marshmallow,
Shimmering like raindrops on roses.
The lake, still, like a leopard waiting to pounce,
This place, as quiet as a sunset on a winter's day . . .

The air hits me, colder than an ice cube,
I am in this worldwide wonderful fridge.
A sparkling dove flies over peacefully.
The naked trees shiver with the coldness of the wind,
This place, so surreal, like the wonderful dream it is.

The sun glows like a fire burning brightly,
Not a sound, but the snowdrops falling with a silent bang.
Suddenly a cloud-surfer,
Circling in the distance,
Swoops, then disappears . . .

Day turns to night and everything fades,
I lie in the snow, take a deep breath and sigh.
I watch the diamonds, sparkling in the night sky,
Watching them I fall asleep,
My eyes close, tired and weary.

Katy Waters (13)
The Downs School, Newbury

I Have A Dream

I have a dream, a dream of colours,
One equal painting of the world at peace

Now, many problems painted in detail
But happiness plain and simple.

A work of art painted in black and white,
None in-between. They meet but never mix,
Created by the dominant ideas,
White in black, black in white, too small to see
A multicoloured dream without racism.

It stands through people like glass in water,
It should not be there at all,
Everyone is different,
Judged on things that do not count.
A dream without prejudice.

Children drop like flies every second,
The hand taking from innocent pockets,
A vacuum going nowhere necessary,
Then the hand of corruption strikes the land
A dream of colours the same shade, equality.

A painting with all colours,
All shades and equal amounts.
I have a dream.

Sophie Preece (12)
The Downs School, Newbury

I Have A Dream . . .

I dream that I will be able to fly,
Like an eagle, soaring above the hills.

I dream that I'll be able to run
Alongside the quickest of animals.

I dream that the picture of the most
Beautiful sunset will stay forever.

I dream of being the reason that you
Are wearing the biggest smile ever seen.

I dream of being on top of the world,
Yet only being on top on a mound.

I dream of being remembered for who
I am, not what they wanted me to be.

I dream of being the only person
Knowing the answer to the question: 'Why?'

I dream one day that one's social status
Will not affect who they are inside.

I dream that being beautiful will come
As naturally as blossoming flowers.

And now I'm awake . . . the dream is over.

Helen Booker (13)
The Downs School, Newbury

I Have A Dream

Her eyes were gazing dreamily,
Awash with a sleepy gaze,
As her eyes moved so longingly,
Summer's night, a pollen haze.

She knew what she wanted to be,
Over the giant hill,
Happiness and equality,
The night was all so calm and still.

Her dreams were sweeping her away
She fell into a sleep,
She saw a world of happiness,
Just a world you'd want to keep.

In the sweet world across the hill,
Whites and blacks were holding hands,
No segregation and no hate,
Everyone loved their fellow man.

She looked down at her stubby hands,
Her hands were chocolate-brown,
She wished the world that she lived in,
Could have love around.

Stephanie Brown (12)
The Downs School, Newbury

Songs Of Past Dreams

I scarce glimpsed, as I peered out through misty panes
of human minds:
A world we all once knew that's now been dumped and left behind.
We know that time has passed, the waves of time still gently break,
Yet abundant shiny pebbles do those ocean waves still make.

Songs of praise and wonder rise up high unto the end;
A day with no beginning, a skyline without an end;
A long, seductive history, we look behind so well:
Tales of mighty warriors but to different swords they fell.

A roughened surface smoothed is worth a hundred bits of glass;
The time for war and peace will soon indeed come to pass.
The treasures of the mind will last, with every step made higher,
And in a distant, hazy dream, we'll find the heartfelt fire.

Sarah Tranter (14)
The Downs School, Newbury

I Have A Dream

The thudding of footsteps are close behind,
Awful thoughts and worries run through my head,
Why me? What have I done to deserve this?
Billy-No-Mates, that's what I get called,
I try to fit in but it doesn't work,
My clothes are cool and I don't wear glasses,
A wall of hate is between them and me,
I try to keep my distance from that wall,
If not, the consequences are deadly,
The footsteps are getting much louder now,
I can feel their hot breath on my neck,
I must go on but my legs are jelly,
I can't go on, they are catching me up,
I cannot bear to think what they will do,
I startle awake in a hot fluster,
I feel the shivers creep through my spine,
Only a dream, the day could bring much worse.

Eleanor Bunn (13)
The Downs School, Newbury

Money

Wouldn't it be nice
To live in a world unaffected by price
Where tenners and fivers and coppers
Did not dictate quality of life?

Wouldn't it be great
If the world contained less hate
Because tenners and fivers and coppers
Were now all completely worthless?

Wouldn't it be less hard
If there were no such things as credit cards
Because tenners and fivers and coppers
Couldn't buy a thing?

Because if the saying is true and
'The love of money is the root of all evil'
Then wouldn't the world be more peaceful
If money was completely irrelevant?

Caroline Pringle (15)
The Downs School, Newbury

Your Dream

Dreams are the specialist things
you can soar on eagles' wings.
Dreams are something to be kept
they're sometimes better than reality.

I have a dream that the world will be one
and then the whole world will have won.
That every child can hold hands
and then sing and dance together.

One child's dreams can change the world
just one dream can lift your spirits.
Your dreams should be shown.
Your dreams should be your life.

Emma Hounsell (13)
The Downs School, Newbury

I Have A Dream

Look at the world that we live in today,
There is litter everywhere you look.
In every park and street corner,
This has to stop; we have to clean our world.

Every city lined with litter,
I look on the floor and see crisp packets.
I look in the sky and see pollution,.
This has to stop; we have to clean our world.

Global warming is a huge problem,
It's destroying the world as I speak.
It's ruining our ancestors' lives,
This has to stop; we have to clean our world.

Our world isn't beautiful anymore,
It's one big rubbish dump everywhere you look.
The sky in cities is like a black hole!
This has to stop; we have to clean our world.

People abuse this world like it's theirs,
I think they should be fined if caught doing this.
They've added to the world's suffering,
So they, so they should suffer themselves.

Our world is completely disgraceful,
But we can clean it and turn it around.
The world gave us a life worth living,
Let's create a world worth living in.

John Morgan (12)
The Downs School, Newbury

I Have A Dream

So many people,
So many lives,
So many personalities,
So many families,
Gone.

So many children,
Have lost their parents,
So many parents,
Have lost their children,
So many people,
Have lost their friends,
So many friends,
Have lost their siblings,
But why?
To cancer.

So many wasted opportunities,
So many wasted potentials,
So many personal wants,
Never fulfilled.

If God is meant to be so good,
Why is He so careless?
If God is meant to be so amazing,
Why does He let this happen?
If God is meant to be able to control everything,
And if God is meant to have created everything,
Why does He kill so many people this way?

So many questions,
So few answers.

Grace Ladds (14)
The Downs School, Newbury

My Dream

I once had a nightmare
That evil forces
Had conquered the world
And were enslaving humans.

The forces were called Hatred,
Disease, Poverty, Grief
And were gradually creeping
Into people's lives.

They slowly slunk inside
And spread from a single tiny flower
On a dark tree of despair
Blossoming outwards and spreading away.

Anchoring their roots in society
Digging deeper into people's minds
Feeding on the goodness
And happiness they found there.

Then, as the goodness inevitably
Faded into the roots of darkness
Its seeds were dispersed throughout the world
Breeding anger and hatred.

The seeds grew into tough vines
Ensnaring people's lives
And tightening their grip
On the suffocating world.

But then I realised that this nightmare
Was the terrible reality of the world
And I have a dream that this will change:
That Poverty, Hatred and Anger will die.

That the evil roots will be wrenched from the Earth
Leaving it free at last.

Katy Burgess (12)
The Downs School, Newbury

The Flowers Of Life

There are but two certainties
In a life on Earth
And can fame stop them?
No, it can't.
For fame is just the stem of one
And the mere seed of the other.

There are but two certainties
In a life on Earth
And can money stop them?
No, it can't
For money is just the stem of one
And the mere seed of the other.

There are but two certainties
In a life on Earth
And nothing can stop them.
No, it can't
As death is one
And greed is the other
You won't do anything
No, you shall not.

But, if the people on Earth,
Can try and change
At least they'll die
Most politely.

Josh Dickins (15)
The Downs School, Newbury

I Have A Dream - Make Them Proud

I have a dream that one day my inspiration will come true,
That as I go through the tunnel the crowd calls my name
And makes my parents proud.
As I sing the anthem with the other seventy thousand fans,
I have the ability to change people's thoughts and feelings,
As my parents sit in the third row up,
They sit there with tears in their eyes, as nervous as me,
As the bands walk off and it just myself and fourteen other guys
Left to battle it out for our country.
The nerves have kicked in,
Now I have two very special fans waiting for me,
For me to make them proud.

Jamie Pincott (16)
The Downs School, Newbury

A Poem For Patriotism

There was once a time,
A time when a man was proud
Of his country,
And to shout out loud,
His patriotic verse or rhyme.

There was once a time,
A time when a man flew the flag
For his country,
But when that flag had turned to a rag,
No more was that rhyme.

But when is that time?
A time to relive that glory -
The glory that his country once had,
And to shout to the heavens surely,
'I am British and glad!'

Robert Taylor (15)
The Downs School, Newbury

I Had A Dream

I had a dream last night
The sun was shining and the sky was blue
The people were laughing,
The people were eating and the people were drinking

I had a dream last night
The air was fresh and the fields were fertile
The people were farming
The people were healthy
The people had homes

I had a dream last night
The rivers were clean and the dead were less
The people were talking
The people were warm and the people had wealth

Then I woke up and the people were sad
The people were hungry
The people were poor.

Tom Meredith (13)
The Downs School, Newbury

Life

Life, life flashes by,
One day after another,
Where does it all go?
Life is what happens,
When you are busy making other plans.
Sleep comes. Sleep goes.
Work, then eat, then work,
Then sleep.

Josh Overton (16)
The Downs School, Newbury

I Have A Dream

I have a dream to have peace on Earth
Someone says something but they just get ignored
A broken tap drips on and on
A plumber comes, but it is beyond repair.

I have a dream that words will be actions,
No more guns, world wars, no violence at all
That tap will be dripping forever into eternity.

I have a dream that the news will be good things
Think of the people who get killed for nothing
We can change it if we stand up and speak up
You will never hear a drip off that tap again.

I have a dream that families won't be hurt
Bodies lying broken like shattered glass
Cleared up with a brush and dumped, worthless
Every drip of that tap is death.

I have a dream that you won't have to say goodbye
No friends or family broken by guns
But those are just dreams
The tap drips on . . .

Katherine Browne (13)
The Downs School, Newbury

I Have A Dream . . .

I have a dream of a perfect day, in a perfect world
On a day where the sun shines high up in the sky,
I have a dream of walking into school
Where everyone is friends and keeping the same rule;
I have a dream.

I have a dream where the world is not polluted,
When we can see the sun dancing behind the poisoned cloud,
I have a dream of countries being normal,
Where people don't have to dress up to look formal;
I have a dream.

I have a dream when men and women are treated equally,
Where we can all stay the same, and not be judged,
I have a dream where money would mean nothing,
Where we could tell if MPs were truly bluffing;
I have a dream.

I have a dream when we can let time pass us by,
When the world just gets along,
I have a dream where poverty was finished,
Where there would be no more tears to cry,
I have a dream.

Nancy Leadley (14)
The Downs School, Newbury

I Have A Dream . . .

I have a dream that there are no such things as enemies,
No such thing as unhappiness and depression,
No such thing as a miserable life!

I have a dream that there are no illnesses,
Nothing to harm us,
And no one will die,
There will be no poverty or cancers,
No hospitals or nurses,
Everyone will be happy and healthy.

My dream for life is for it to be like a really good book,
The more you read,
The more you want to find out,
And if you don't continue reading,
You'll never find out what happens in the end!

Life at the minute is a roller coaster,
First of all, you don't know what to expect to get out of it,
And all at once, you reach a really high point and you're excited,
Then before you know it,
You're swooping down, and just as you think that the ride
                                    can't get any worse . . .

It finishes, blinking before your eyes!

Stacy Mills (13)
The Downs School, Newbury

I Have A Dream

I have a dream, that one day I could go
To the place I have always dreamed of.
A place that everyone dreams about,
Except I want it more than anyone.
I yearn for the chance, I want it most.

I have a dream, that one day I could go
To the place that would make me so special.
A place that would change my life forever.
The fire in my heart makes me want it more,
I want it so bad it blazes inside me.

I have a dream, that one day I could go
To a place that I would die to go to.
A place where your worries disappear
And you only care about one small thing.
And I want it more than anything else.

I have a dream, that one day I could go
To the place that is only for the best.
And I am fixated on being the best.
I know I can and I will do anything,
Anything to get to the Olympics.

Arland Craik (13)
The Downs School, Newbury

I Have A Dream

I have a dream, or is it a nightmare?
I awake in the night because of it.
It depicts the end of the world, and us.
The dream is Hell's fires scorching the Earth.

Nuclear power is out of control.
Hell's flames powering death and destruction,
They call them Nukes eating away the Earth.
Great craters of death they cause our planet.

Money is corrupting the big countries.
They suck it from the poor Third World countries.
It's like they burn money instead of wood.
They always need money for something.

The suffering of others is my dream.
The destruction of the Earth is my dream.
Corruption of governments is my dream.
This dream of mine is more of a nightmare.

Joshua Booth (13)
The Downs School, Newbury

I Have A Dream

. I have a dream that one day there will be no conflicts.
I have a dream that everyone will live in peace.
I have a dream to change the world.
I have a dream that no one's dream is ever too big.
I dream that there will be no more bombings.
I dream that there will be no unnecessary loss of life.
I have the dream where there is no chance of nuclear war.
I have the dream where there is no famine.
I have dreams that make me believe that we can change.
I have dreams that there will be no pain.
I have dreams and dreams make us who we are
The dreams we have can one day change the world!

Jessica Smith (16)
The Downs School, Newbury

I Have A Dream

I dream that it is the end of the world
And every tale is over.
Silence as everyone realises their fate
Followed by cries and screams of devastation.

The sky once a beautiful blue, turns now to grey
From my roof, I can see everything for miles
Yet I can see no sign of life.

No birds flying in the sky
No fish jumping in the river
No cows grazing in the fields
Only death, disaster and despair.

Fires burning with fury and menace
Rain beginning to pour down
A zigzag of a lightning bolt
And a great crash of thunder.

Holly Kettlewell (13)
The Downs School, Newbury

I Have A Dream

I am inspired by sportsmen
who overcome illness
and then go on to achieve great things
and overcome the odds.
Lance Armstrong inspires me,
a man that had cancer and
had months to live, then went on
to win seven Tour de France races.
My dreams are that the world
can live in peace and tranquillity
and that everyone eats ketchup!

Martin J Raisey (16)
The Downs School, Newbury

This Is My Dream

Take my hand, tell me what to believe,
As if there is only one way to see.
The faith you choose might not be for me,
How can I be saved, while being forced to believe?

So try and save the world one by one,
Try and make them believe what you think is wrong,
They can't question what they've been told,
Try and make them believe, try and save the world.

So spread the word, announce the good news,
That if we act this way, we can be like you.
To live is to learn and think for yourself,
I can do that without any help.

This is my dream, to be like no one else,
To savour my faith and make my own wealth.
My thoughts and feelings won't be dictated to me,
I'll make my own path and sow my own seeds.

Harriet Dipple (15)
The Downs School, Newbury

My Horse Dream

I wish I had a horse with a gold and silver mane,
as a friend of mine had one exactly the same.
I would have one if I could rake up the cash,
I feed my own horse on corn and mash.
Whatever the outcome, I would not be sad,
as my own horse is a very good lad.
It's very hard to pick and choose,
I have not got the money but have not got the blues!

Becky Smith (11)
The Downs School, Newbury

I Have A Dream . . .

I have a dream that . . .

H atred between countries, races and religions will end.
A ll people will have food, homes and happiness.
V olatile situations will be calmed with words not war.
E ducation will be given to everyone.

A mbitions will not be crushed by race or status.

D octors will find cures to the terrible diseases that ruin our lives.
R eality will be like dreams and dreams will be reality
E arth will survive all ravages of mankind and bounce back to life.
A nd, lastly, I dream that . . .
M y dream will come true.

Rebecca Smith (13)
The Downs School, Newbury

I Have A Dream

Sometimes I just want to get right up
And spread my arms to Heaven above
To feel the sparkling sun warm my face
And smell the sweet, spring grass and clean daisies.
I want to grow something wild and free,
I want to look at the world from above
And not see a building standing tall.
I want to run, not caring about cars.
I just want to stand on the horizon
And feel the wind in my hair and face.
This is my dream, this is all I want
For the horizon is the end of the world.
People ridicule me for saying this.
They say the horizon is not the end
But it is and always will be for me
Because my world ends at the horizon
For all I can see is the horizon.

Emma Sanderson (13)
The Downs School, Newbury

Dreams Of Mine

I have dreams, I make dreams, I live dreams
These are my dreams
I hope the world lives my dreams.

I have dreams where slavery is a myth
I make dreams where people don't have to suffer
I live dreams like peace and love

I have dreams, I make dreams, I live dreams
These are my dreams
I hope the world lives my dreams too

I have dreams where hunger lingers no more
I make dreams where everyone is happy
I live my life like a dream
I hope you are with me there.

Jack Birtwistle (12)
The Downs School, Newbury

I Have A Dream . . .

I can see the world,
Not today and not tomorrow
But one day I can see the world, free and
'Nobody need wait a single moment
Before starting to improve the world!'
Now is the time to start,
Forty years ago was the time to start . . .
'Because life is what happens
When you are busy making other plans.'
The past has gone, forgotten.
The future, however, is now!
Life is now;
So, for that one day, we must start,
Now!

Alice Wilson (16)
The Downs School, Newbury

I Have A Dream

I have a dream of undeniable joy,
Where my sons and daughters are playing with their toys.
How I got there's a story to tell.
To get to Heaven I had to walk through Hell.

One night I finished a gig with my band.
A guy came up and said we'd be grand.
We signed his contract and then we were off
Around the world with no more than a cough.

When we got back we were rich and well-known
In papers and letters, we were glad to be home.
Alas one night, our guitarist died.
His funeral, my best friend, his daughter, my bride.

Will Madgwick (15)
The Downs School, Newbury

I Have A Dream

Inspiration is a flowing stream
of clear liquid finding its way
over pebbles and rocks
bubbling and gushing down
a gentle slope, with
the warm morning sun
bursting through gaps in tall
oak tree leaves, casting
patterned shadows upon the
sanded banks as a tranquil sound
of birds singing penetrates
the all but silent surroundings.
A perfect rainbow of natural
colours, reds, brown, yellows,
greens, ,whites and blues, all rush
into my eyes.

Ryan Gulless (15)
The Downs School, Newbury

I Have A Dream

I have a dream,
A dream that could come true,
If people would just try,
Instead of watching others die!

I have a dream,
That the world would be a better place,
A better place for people
Of each and every different race!

I have a dream,
Another dream that would come true,
If people would stop fighting their brothers
And start making peace with others!

My dreams really would
Come true,
If people really wanted
Them to!

Isla Birnie (13)
The Downs School, Newbury

I Have A Dream

I have a dream that we will make poverty history
That we will stop the world hunger
That we will feed the world
But it's only us, who will make this happen.

I have a dream that we will kick racism out of the world
That the world's people will be sheltered
That terrorism will stop
But it's only us, who will make this happen.

I have a dream that criminals were all captured
That famine stopped
That everyone lived in peace and harmony
But it's only us who will make this happen.

Sam King (13)
The Downs School, Newbury

I Have A Dream . . .

I dream of a world where no one is poor,
No beggars or tramps come knocking at your door,
The famine in Africa has gone away,
And everyone earns above minimum pay.

I dream of a world where no one is ill,
Where you don't have injections or swallow a pill,
Where cancer is cured and flu has fled,
And nobody dies in a hospital bed.

I dream of a world where no one gets hurt,
No countries are bombed and no houses are burnt,
Suicide jumpers step back from the edge,
And terrorist bombers are friendly instead.

Unfortunately, none of this is true,
People get shot and infected with flu,
People get starved and people get sick
And it's not going to stop unless we do something
Quick!

Oliver Rigg (13)
The Downs School, Newbury

I Have A Dream

I have a dream that one day I will play for England
and score a hat trick in the World Cup Final!

I have a dream

I have a dream that one day I will play in the 2012
Olympic Games and win a gold medal.

I have a dream

I have a dream that I will represent my country
and break and set a world record that nobody will ever break.

I have a dream.

Edward Ardill (13)
The Downs School, Newbury

A World Without . . .

I have a dream,
I heard them say,
A world without war,
And minimum wage,

We'll stand and fight,
For what we believe,
Without weapons and death,
And war on parade,

A world without famine,
And Third World debt,
Killing is the game,
The government win,

But who wants to play this game?
Who wants to kill?
The innocent people,
Our pockets they fill.

Ben Hordos (15)
The Downs School, Newbury

I Have A Dream

I have a dream that there will be no wars,
Diseases destroyed and aid to all who need it,

Poverty will be stopped in all places,
Help and shelter to those who don't have it,

Poorer countries set free from their debt to rich countries,
Proper justice for all.

This is my dream!

James Atkins (13)
The Downs School, Newbury

No One Man Can Move Mountains

No one man can stop poverty,
No one man can stop wars,
No one man can stop suffering,
No one man can stop droughts,
No one man can stop global warming,
No one man can stop diseases,
No one man can repay world debt,
No one man can move mountains.

But man together can stop poverty, wars and suffering,
We can stop droughts, global warming and disease,
Debts can be repaid.

No one man can move mountains,
But if every one of us in this world,
Took a part of all our problems . . .

We may be able to live in peace.

Rauraidh Purnell (14)
The Downs School, Newbury

I Had A Dream

I had a dream that bird flu
Killed everybody from China to Peru,
Even the animals in the zoo
And nobody knew what to do.

The scientists will have to make a pill
To stop us all from feeling ill,
Hope the scientists are quick
To make a pill so we are not sick.

I like my life, I don't want to die
Every day I cry and cry,
Then I wake, it was a dream
But it's really happening over the sea
So they had better hurry up!

Joshua Hadland (12)
The Downs School, Newbury

My Perfect Day

I wake up on my perfect day,
the sun is shining,
which makes me happy and gay.

My mum walks in with toast and jam,
cup of tea and a talk about
her friends that are coming round.

The phone starts to ring,
Mum runs down,
she calls up to me and
tells me someone is coming round.

I have a shower
and then start to get dressed,
my mum shouts up,
'Charleigh put on your best.'

The doorbell rings
I hear my name
I run down the stairs
and shout, 'Hooray!'

Lizzie McGuire is standing there,
she says, 'Hello' and gives me a smile.
All I remember about that day
Is that it was my perfect day.

Charleigh Bailey (12)
The Downs School, Newbury

I Have A Dream!

I have a dream,
That will never be true.

I dream that when I wake up,
The world will be perfect.
But I know it won't.

I have a dream,
I have a dream,
That will never be true.

I dream when I wake up,
There'll be no wars.
But I know people will always fight.

I have a dream,
I have a dream,
I have a dream,
That will never be true.

I dream when I wake up,
There will be no hunger or thirst,
But I know people cause it by greed.

I have a dream,
I have a dream,
I have a dream,
I have a dream,
That will never come true.

I dream when I wake up,
Animals will all be safe and happy.
But I know we will always hurt them.

I have a dream,
I have a dream,
I have a dream,
I have a dream,
I have a dream,
That will only come true if we pull together.

I have a dream,
That might come true
I have a dream,
That could come true.

Beth Rutterford (13)
The Downs School, Newbury

This Is My Dream

I have a dream
That one day Man will
Conquer the universe;
That we will move on
To worlds far better
Than our own.

This is my dream.

I have a dream
That all our manual labour
Will be done by machines;
That space travel will be
Accessible for everyone.

This is my dream.

I have a dream
That when we look up at
The night sky, we will be able
To reach to the most distant star
With relative ease.

That is my dream.

Robert Ensor (14)
The Downs School, Newbury

Perfect Days . . .

One day life will run smoothly,
we will all be successful and find an inner talent.
I have a dream . . .

Children will get a good education,
grow up, get a job and have a family
I have a dream . . .

Animals will have a free life,
like a butterfly, be free and have their own time
I have a dream . . .

The environment will be clean and healthy,
and people will leave it be; other than to care for it
I have a dream . . .

People will care for each other,
stop fighting and look into each other's eyes and
respect
one another and listen to each other's points of view
I have a dream . . .

I have a dream of perfect days
This would inspire anyone
I have a dream . . .

Leanne Spencer (12)
The Downs School, Newbury

I Have A Dream

Everybody dreams
Of things they desire.
Of peace and prosperity,
Of freedom and equality,
Or most do.

There are some who would
Demolish a dream.
Some who strive to be superior,
Because of the colour of your skin.

Why colour? It is hardly any different
To wearing black clothes instead of white.
What if nobody had skin?
What then - discriminating the colour of one's muscles?
Or one's nerves - more to the point.

So why all this hate?
Why all this anger?
Why all this mistrust?
Why all this discrimination?

There are those who believe the
End of the world
Is almost upon us.

And indeed it will be, unless
We stop sitting on our rears,
And stand up, and take action.
And make our bodies perform
The deeds our mouths speak of.

That is my dream.

Isabella Kildonan (13)
The Downs School, Newbury

She Has A Dream . . .

She has a dream . . .
She's had it since she was a little girl,
She really hopes it will come true,
She wishes on every shooting star,
She wants to win an Olympic gold medal.

She has a dream . . .
She so badly wants it to come true,
She works so hard to achieve it,
She loves her running,
She will never give up.

She has a dream . . .
She knows it will be difficult,
She looks up to those like Kelly Holmes,
She knows hardly any people who became Olympic champions,
She really believes in herself.

She has a dream . . .
She's been told she has talent,
She has her own coach to guide her,
She won't let anything get in her way,
She has to work hard.

She has a dream . . .

Will she ever accomplish her dream?

Amanda Nevill (13)
The Downs School, Newbury

To Never See A Blue Sky

I have a dream
I have a thought
That cruelty to animals will never be bought

I have a dream
That we really ought
To make factory farming come to a nought

Facts hidden by
Commercialisation
Facts that are completely ignored by the nation:

These facts being awful
These facts filled with dread
One being locked in a cage, in a shed

One thinks of the sky
As something taken for granted
The colour of blue, so disenchanted

But to never see
A clear blue sky
Is something amazingly, remarkably vile.

I have a dream
I have a thought
That we should give creatures a share of our lot.

Samuel Rees (11)
The Downs School, Newbury

Their Dream

Think about your life, your wants and your needs,
Think about your dreams, your nightmares and your thoughts,
Are they about wealth, love and eternal happiness?
Are they small or big, to live long, lasting love or a big feed?
Take a moment, sit down, close your eyes and put your life on pause
Take a silent moment in your sleep and your mind, the mess.

To change the world has to start by changing your thoughts,
To see the world as it really is, has to start by changing your sight,
Do you see the children on the street, eyes full of fear?
Do you see that limp body in the box, restless on the train
as it departs?
Can you hear a baby screaming as it crawls into the light?
Can you hear that woman's breath, short, desperate,
as the fog begins to clear?

Could you live your life, knowing there is no reason?
Could you wake up every day, to hear another body flop?
To crawl instead of walk; starve instead of eat; their lives are on loan
To fight instead of sleep; die instead of wake; death is on their
shoulders through every season
They live for today, there is no tomorrow. When will the Devil stop?
They inspire me, the people who live in Hell; who starve in droughts
and who die unknown.

Who are they? Where are they? You might ask,
They are on the streets every night but no one knows their name,
They are on the television every day but they are not famous,
They are all around; they are our future; our present; our past.
They are the people that cried all night, but no comfort ever came.
They are the homeless, the helpless, the dead, and the starved
yet never make a fuss.

Think what their hopes, wants and dreams are
To eat this month; to drink this week; to live this day.
Every day they work without money; sleep without beds; and die
without family,
However, we drown in our money; lie tired on our beds;
and love our families who live afar,
If we are ill, we can be cured; if we are hungry we can eat; if they
are ill or hungry; all they can do is pray,
Their dream is but to be free.

Chloé Trigg (14)
The Downs School, Newbury

I Have A Dream . . .

I have a dream that one day,
I will be an astronomer,
Looking up into the big blue sky studying the stars
As if watching different species of fish swim by.

I have a dream that I will sit outside,
Sitting on a chair and looking through my telescope,
Staring hard at the sky, feeling that I am drowning in a dark sea.
While I'm drowning, I may even discover what the future holds for us.

I have a dream, that I will learn physics
Perfectly,
That I may even become a physics teacher
And inspire other people to become one too,
As there are many young talented astronomers out there.
Stand up for my position and say physics will not be demolished
From schools across the country.

Devna Birdi (13)
The Downs School, Newbury

Do You Have A Dream Today?

Be a spaceman, army man,
policeman, bin man

Win the Olympics, write a book,
go skydiving, be a cook

Build a skyscraper, climb a mountain,
become a millionaire, jump in a fountain

Re-invent yourself, clone yourself,
discover yourself, *be* yourself

Start a charity, turn a life around,
discover something amazing, something profound

Prevent racism, be a light in dark times,
stop terrorism, solve all the world's crimes

Save a life, plant a tree,
witness a miracle, set someone free

End all suffering, make poverty cease,
find a cure for cancer, create world peace

No one knows just what the future holds
whatever you do, dream.

Do you have a dream today?

Pippy Wiseman (14)
The Downs School, Newbury

I Have A Dream

I have a dream that the guns will drop,
the war will end,
the fighting will stop.

I have a dream that the killing will end,
we will all unite,
and make a new friend.

I have a dream that the shooting will halt,
we can do it,
we can be kind without fault.

I have a dream that friendship will bloom,
don't worry people,
there will be happiness soon.

Oscar Roper (12)
The Downs School, Newbury

I Have A Dream . . .

As I lie here in this hospital bed,
No ring on my finger,
A heart full of lead,

I have a dream.

I dream that I was not led astray.
Not bound into smoking every day.

I have a dream,

That my soul was clear.
No sins to admit to,
Or worries to fear.

But no matter how much I dream,
These wishes cannot come true,
As I have wasted my life,
Have you?

Emma McCarthy (12)
The Downs School, Newbury

I Have A Dream

Pure, to start unknown
To be in the background
Stay where nobody goes
Be alone
Be with your thoughts
Step into the sun.
You're out of the dark.
But are they ready?
You start to speak . . .
They have to listen.
Your silence has not made you bitter,
It has made you think *bliss!*
Pure bliss.
Pure ownage.
Jeremy (the owner) stepped into the light.
They listened to him.
He helped them.
Purely an inspiration.

Daniel Rowbotham (15)
The Downs School, Newbury

I Have A Dream

I have a dream that one day all people of the world
will live together in peace and harmony.

I have a dream that some day terrorism
will finally be beaten once and for all.

I have a dream that every good person
will live a long, happy, fulfilled life.

I have a dream that one day I will score the winning goal
in the World Cup Final for England.

I have a dream that the world will pull together
to stop poverty and global warming before it is too late.

Rory Holliday (12)
The Downs School, Newbury

I Have A Dream

I have a dream that love will overcome,
that war will end,
and that families will feel at one.

My dream is not simple,
but yet is it hard?
Everybody in the world should begin to start,

I have a dream that flowers will blossom,
grief will cease,
and healing will happen.

World leaders will unite,
countries will sing in harmony,
and evil people in the world will stop their fight.

I have a dream,
although it is small,
my un-simple dream,
could change it all.

Daisy McDowell (13)
The Downs School, Newbury

I Have A Dream

I have a dream that one day there will be no racism in the world.
I have a dream that one day terrorists will throw away their guns.
I have a dream that we can make poverty history.
I have a dream that scientists can find a cure for diseases.
I have a dream that there will be no crime in the world.
I have a dream that we can stop global warming and polluting.
I have a dream that there will be no Third World countries.
I have a dream that Tottenham will win the Premiership.

Jack Moates (12)
The Downs School, Newbury

Slow Down The World

Rushes of colour,
in a changing world,
a wave of noise.
Frustrated they storm by,
wanting every moment to count as though
they might die.
Their world is spinning faster,
everyone's in a rush,
to get stardom status,
more money
and a job.
When will they stop being blinded
by empty promises of fame?
When will they take time to stop this stupid game?
When will they hear the haunting cries
of starved children in Africa,
the young girl that dies?
When will they see what the world really is?
They only need to help one step at a time,
to slow down the world and regain time.

Rachel Dalton (14)
The Downs School, Newbury

I Have A Dream

Their skin is black
They get no flack
Their hair is red
But nothing is said
They may have freckles
But get no heckles
This could come true
If it weren't for the mindless few.

Sam Wheeler (12)
The Downs School, Newbury

The Perfect Recipe For World Peace

First of all you need some bravery,
Use scales of peace to measure the gravy,
After that pour in Mandela,
Then add some given bread from the cellar.

And for the main course you need some John Lennon,
This then should be seasoned with some trust and lemon,
And then for the taste, add Martin Luther King,
Political guidance this will bring.

And then for dessert, add some chilled Anne Frank,
Which should be coated with hope and fried in a pan,
And for the second part add some Albert Einstein,
Once you've added that this recipe will be defined.

There are some good ingredients,
It is a better recipe,
But imagine everyone that loving,
What a perfect world this would be.

Jessica Chorley (12)
The Downs School, Newbury

I Have A Dream

I have a dream but when I wake up, it will not be true.
In my dream there are no fights,
The Earth is like a light.
In my dream there is no war,
No one wants more.
In my dream we live in peace,
There is no need for police,
But that is all just a dream.

George Marffy (11)
The Downs School, Newbury

I Have A Dream

I have a dream
of a perfect world,
where everything is just right.
I have a dream
of a perfect day,
One that lasts through till the night.
I have a vision
a vision of love,
spread around the Earth.
I have a vision
a vision of Nirvana,
where no one is treated like dirt.
Is there a chance
of eternal peace,
With no discrimination or war?
Is there a chance
that we can all fight
for something worth fighting for?
I see a light
a light of hope,
that we can all get along.
I see a light
a light of hope,
where we can work together in song.

Johnathan Worley (15)
The Downs School, Newbury

I Have A Dream

I have a dream
That one day
In the world I'll see
Peace and prosperity
For all to be
I have a dream
That one day
The world will be a better place
Filled with love and grace
No sighs, but smiles
Just friends, not foes

I hope I'll see
No walls or class
That all people
Will be as one
No north, no south
No east, no west
No differences between the rest
The world is troubled
That I can see
My dream,
The world I'll hope to see.

Charlotte Oldroyd (13)
The Downs School, Newbury

I Have A Dream . . .

I have a dream . . .
That there will be world peace.

What would the world be like with no
bullying or racism?
No murders,
no hatred,
no violence,
no harassment,
no abuse.
Will there ever be world peace?

What would the world be like without
any wars?
No guns,
no bombs,
no dying,
no weapons,
no killing.
Will there ever be world peace?

Nicola Willock (11)
The Downs School, Newbury

Stop Smoking!

It's always there, lurking around.
Up near the ceiling, down near the ground.
It's evil, it chokes and sometimes kills,
Can be stopped with gum or nicotine pills,
The victims are anyone who takes one of these,
It makes you cough hard, not just a sneeze,
Don't even start it, it's really hard to stop.
People bribe you, say that it's cool but really it's not.

Rebecca Ebdon Taylor (12)
The Downs School, Newbury

I Have A Dream

One person who moves mountains
One person tries to change
But if it all goes wrong
Then there's only one to blame

If the world unites
Then those mountains can be moved
If the dream is spoken
Maybe it will come true

I have a dream
That we all will stand united
If poverty is real
Then maybe we should fight it

This is my dream
The world will be as one
When poverty is history
Then our work is done.

Madeline Wilding (13)
The Downs School, Newbury

My Dream

I have a dream that one day
I can swim for England in the 2012 Olympics
If I have my way
Just like Ian Thorpe or Katy Sexton

I have a dream that one day
A clinical psychologist I'll be
Mums and dads I'll help to play
With their children
Come what may
Just like Tanya Bryan

I have a dream that one day
I can be a volunteer
Looking after the elderly, disabled and animals
That will be a way
To be like my mum, sister and dad.

I'm really glad
That I have a dream.
That I have a dream.

Sarah Hubbard (13)
The Downs School, Newbury

I Have A Dream

I have a dream,
To fly up high,
Soar above everything,
With the clouds in the sky.

I have a dream,
To fly with the birds,
To see further than anyone,
It's just too fun for words.

I have a dream,
To fly above the trees,
To glide above everything,
On land and in sea.

I have a dream,
I know it's not true,
That is my dream,
What about you?

Danielle Fisher (12)
The Downs School, Newbury

I Have A Dream . . .

I have a dream and as I dream,
I dream dreamily of,
Something that is no reality,
A place of no disease,
Where everyone is at ease,
And global warming is no more.

As I dream through the dreamy haze I see,
Eternal life,
No guns or knives,
No violence whatsoever,
This is a world of equals.

I'm having a dream of
Winning the lottery,
Where things aren't too scary,
I can fly,
There is no debt in this world.

I have a dream, but it is only a dream,
A dream is not reality,
Through the dreaming I awake,
And the dream is no more.

Mirren Kessling (12)
The Downs School, Newbury

I Have A Dream

I have a dream,
An impossible, unimaginable dream,
A dream of peace on Earth,
Of equal rights no matter who you are,
Of governments ending Third World debt.

Of support to those in need,
Of aid to those who suffer,
Of help to those in trouble,
This is my dream.

A dream of ending poverty,
Of saving lives through medicine,
Of giving the homeless a place to live,
Of anger and hatred to be forgotten,
Of love and happiness for all.

This is my dream,
My possible, imaginable dream,
My dream of peace,
Of togetherness,
Make my dreams come true.

Amanda Walsh (12)
The Downs School, Newbury

I Have A Dream

As I lie here, thinking,
I gaze into the trees.
My face cooled by the crisp autumn breeze.
Something ignites, the whole world blinking
In surprise.

The trees explode in a burst of light,
Then, drifting in the water,
A lady comes and says, 'You are a fairy's daughter.'
I stand, rooted to the spot,
In surprise.

The adventure starts, my mind whirling,
Beautiful dresses for dancing and twirling.
Unicorns' spells, magic and castles,
Then a portal to take me back home
Standing, in surprise.

As I lie here, thinking,
I gaze into the trees.
My face cooled by the crisp autumn breeze.
I had a dream, and fulfilled it.
Surprise, surprise, surprise.

Kirsten Hunter (11)
The Downs School, Newbury

I Have A Dream

I have a dream
That I can fly
Over the seas and in the sky
I can walk on water
Jump on the clouds
Run around school being really loud

I have a dream
That I can save
Everyone that got hit by the wave
On Boxing Day 2004
But I can't help them anymore

I have a dream
That I can save lives
Making poverty history
And help people stay alive

I have a dream
That sweets are healthy
And that I am very wealthy
That I have a plane for me and my friends
And that my childhood never ends.

Emily Gadd (11)
The Downs School, Newbury

I Have A Dream

I have a dream to travel,
To travel near and far,
To discover hidden lands,
Or maybe a brand new star.

I have a dream to travel,
By plane, or train, or boat,
Sunshine, rain or snow,
I just hope we stay afloat.

The world lies before you,
Its mysteries concealed,
By mountain, sea and shore,
More will be revealed.

My dream lies in the hidden land,
Its secrets not yet told.
I know not what awaits me,
But I only hope it's gold.

I have a dream to watch the wildlife,
In their natural habitat,
Hear the squawk of a parrot,
And the roar of a big cat.

So my dreams are all planned out,
And I hope they do come true,
For I want to see the world,
And travel to places new.

Dominique Bailey (13)
The Downs School, Newbury

I Have A Dream - Bullying

A child sits alone in the corner,
listening to the laughter that cuts into her mind
like the knives she uses to punish herself
for the never-ending guilt she holds inside.

A young man sits alone in the corner,
searching his mind for a reason to tell his parents
why his legs are again covered in bruises.

A girl cries in the corner trying to think of
an explanation for why someone would destroy
all her hope and not seem to care . . .

I have a dream that one day these children
will be understood by their peers for who they are.

I have a dream where these children
have somewhere to go and someone to talk to
to release their worry.

I have a dream where every person
is considered as equal and not judged
by the clothes they wear,
or the style of their hair,
or the colour of their skin,
or if they're fat or they're thin.

'How wonderful it is that nobody need wait a single moment
before starting to improve the world!'

Emily Brooke (14)
The Downs School, Newbury

Perfect

We all have things to hide. We know what has been tried.
I know I should expose everything that is inside.
But the question that plagues us is can we open our lives . . . ?

I'll open my door and with this I let you in:

Don't try to tell me that your life feels empty,
All there is to come is no hope for tomorrow, for today.
We've become children of paralysed ambition,
A fraction less human, pre-packaged warmth,
Arrested ambition. You can sit down but the chairs are electric.

All this reliance on modern technology,
Why not rip down the buildings, bulldoze the architect
And the biased opinions from outdated intellect?

Inspiration has been diluted and we keep sailing with the fear
of falling.

If I had a dream,
It would be to check out and enlist for stable living.
So let's drop the act, I've found something more appealing:
Live each day like it is your last and love yourself, the world
around you,
And all the complications that come with it.

Heads hung over toilets, desperate to achieve the image
of perfection,
Arms scarred crimson with cuts and slashes, crying out for attention.
These are such sorry sights.

For you should not look for all the negativity in the world
But strive to reach your maximum potential as a person.
There is no such thing as 'perfect'
Every person has created themselves, they are the reflection of their
Own thoughts and beliefs, as each of us think and believe, so we are.
If you don't stand for yourself, then you don't stand for much.

Ourselves and the world may not be pure, but we're not all that toxic.
For there is hope for tomorrow, for today.

Christina Goulding (15)
The Downs School, Newbury

The World Looks Brighter From Behind A Smile

Whenever I feel like the world is full of hate and anger,
Whenever I see news of war or devastation on the TV,
I think about the café I go to most Saturdays for lunch.

Hundreds of people walk through the doors every day
With their friends and families; husbands and wives,
Young lovers, old lovers, mothers and daughters, fathers and sons.
Despite the eclectic mix of personas among the customers,
They all have one thing in common.

The little reflex which widens the mouth, lifts the cheeks,
Brightens the eyes, and moves the world for a whole moment.
They smile. And they smile. They smile, they smile . . .
And they're smiling too.

How can there really be pain, when sat across a table is your
                                        best friend?
How can there really be hate when from behind the smeared
Brim of a coffee cup, he looks deep into your eyes and says
With such conviction that he loves you?
How can there be doubt when a smile of perfect happiness is
                                        plastered across your face?

Then I begin to do it too. I feel the warmth radiating from my mouth,
The sunlight from my cheery eyes bathes my vision in laughter,
I see the beauty of the rainy sky and the wilting flowers,
And I am safe in the knowledge that in a café a few miles away,
Other people are in love with life too.

Lois Haines (14)
The Downs School, Newbury

A Dream, A Wish, An Ambition

A dream is a wish that fills our heart,
A journey we must take,
A destiny we must fulfil.
A wish is a want, a longing,
Something that might not be possible,
But if you wish hard enough, it will seem real to you.
An ambition is a desire, a milestone,
A goal which you feel you need to achieve.
I have an ambition, well, it's more of a dream,
To own my own restaurant, and cook for the greats,
To show up Oliver, out-swear Ramsey,
And impress all of my mates.
I would call my restaurant 'Gubb's Grub',
This would flash in neon light,
People would come from all around,
To stop off and grab a bite.

Alex Gubb (13)
The Downs School, Newbury

I Have A Dream

I have a dream that one day, either soon or far,
I will find some happiness,
That the world will become a united place,
That we can look at people and behind all the bad
See the good in people,
That we can recognise who is hurting before it's too late,
And each country of the world can look to its neighbours
For help and support, not the war and terror that exists today.
I hope that everyone in this world finds someone to look up to,
Finds someone that loves them as much as they love them,
As in this world everyone needs someone to confide in,
And needs somebody to need them!

Helen Beasley (16)
The Downs School, Newbury

Bullying!

Bullying is in any place or in any environment
Bullying has an effect like no other.

Bullying has an effect that no one can explain
It can happen to anyone or any child.

If you are one of them, think again.
Just imagine if you were that person
And then you would understand.

If you are sitting back, watching it happen
Get up and try and help them.
Tell someone, give them some advice, help them.
It feels like you are a red flag
And a bull is charging at you.
Would you like that?
Think . . . it can be stopped!

Carl Pomfret (13)
The Downs School, Newbury

I Have A Dream

I have a dream that one day
the sun will shine from the sky.
All the children will run outside
screaming with joy and happiness.
When I'm older I want to see my
children running around with joy
and screaming with happiness.
I want to see my children grow old.
I want to see my children's children.
But that's only a dream.
I want to see it come true.

Ben Revell (12)
The Downs School, Newbury

I Have A Dream

I have a dream.
Isn't it lush to sit and watch the day go by
While you lie?
I love to dream, it lets me believe in me.
I have many dreams and hopefully I will be able to achieve.
Isn't it lush to sit in the sun
And let your hair down?
I love to dream so that I can be wherever I want to be.
Wherever that place may be, all I know is that I can be free.
Isn't it lush to be with the one you love?
No care in the world as to what that person may have done.
Sit, talk, cuddle or snore.
All I know is that I will never let you go.

So dream, dream, no dream is ever too small
So please, please, do not give up.

Rhian James (16)
The Downs School, Newbury

My Words To Change The World

I have a dream that all people who are different
Will be treated the same.
No more racism or discrimination.
When I am older I wish that the world will be peaceful,
As peaceful as a warm, summer night.
I want to see my children grow old.
See them grow up, not die before me.
I have a dream that one day I will be able to knock out racism
                                            for good.

I believe that all terrorist attacks should end.
I wish that all cruelty to people should stop.
I have a dream which one day will come true.

Joseph Faloona (13)
The Downs School, Newbury

Dreaming

Dreaming to save the world
From global warming and poverty.
Saving people's lives
And helping them survive.

Dreaming to make poverty history
By raising money to give people help,
So they can stay alive.

Dreaming that I can save people's lives
By giving food and clothes,
Then they might not feel as sad
And their lives they will not loathe.

Dreaming to change the things people do,
Fighting never stops,
People die every day,
As they do not have a home.
They cannot earn a living,
But you could help by giving.

Food and clothes and maybe money
Could help change someone's life.
Money could build a shelter!
Just a blanket could keep someone warm!
These small things could help a life
And keep someone alive!

Dreaming to do something for me!
Jump into a pool of gold,
Fly up high in the sky,
Run around and never stop,
Never growing old.

Hollie Richardson (11)
The Downs School, Newbury

I Have A Dream

I have a dream to see what no one else has seen,
I have a dream to be where no one else has been.

Maybe you have a dream
To meet the Queen,
To fly a spaceship,
To take a great trip.

I have a dream to see what no one else has seen,
I have a dream to be where no one else has been.

Can you design a video game?
Surely you don't want the world to stay the same.
Are you worried about the environment?
What do you want to be different?

I have a dream to see what no one else has seen,
I have a dream to be where no one else has been.

Your dream can come true,
But only if you want it to.
One day you could fly,
But only if you try!

Jeff Vinall (11)
The Downs School, Newbury

Dreams . . .

I have a dream
That when I am old,
My grandchildren will ask me,
'What is war?'
Not having lived in a time where one is happening.

I have a dream
That in the future,
Malnourished children will not be starving,
Dehydrated and dying
On the desert plains of Africa.

I have a dream
That some day
Poverty will not exist
And children will not be diseased with AIDS
Before they have reached their teens.

I have a dream
That my dreams will become reality,
Because nothing is impossible,
Nothing is beyond our ability.
Whilst I sit here writing this poem,
Thousands of children are dying,
We need to do something to stop poverty,
Now.

Hannah Goulding (12)
The Downs School, Newbury

I Have A Dream

I have a dream,
A dream of tomorrow,
A dream for the future,
A dream for life.

Imagine love shared equally,
Imagine hope for everyone,
Imagine peace and friendship
With not just mother and daughter, father and son.
Imagine a united world
With everybody equal.

No poverty to prevent us,
No doubts on people's minds,
No prejudice to harm us,
Just love and friendship binds.

A perfect world, a perfect place,
Laughter, friendship and love
For everyone, everywhere, forever.

Molly Geach (11)
The Downs School, Newbury

One Day

One day I want the world to be peaceful,
I want everyone to live a long and fruitful life,
No matter what crimes they have committed.

One day I want poverty to be washed away,
Not just in the places you'd expect there to be,
But in places like the UK and USA.

One day I want the world to be in beautiful harmony,
No global warming, no pollution, absolutely nothing!

One day I don't want to see people crammed in tiny shelters of tin,
I want to see them all under a roof of love and prosperity.

I do not want to see people suffering in high debt,
Neither do I want to see unfairness, but instead loving care.

No bullying! No racists!
The world will be heaven!

Tom Smith (12)
The Downs School, Newbury

I Have A Dream

I have a dream of meeting Will Smith,
He's dreamy and he's fit,
He isn't one bit like Brad Pitt.

When I go and see him,
He'll be singing on the stage
And he won't at all have aged.

He will see me in the crowd
And he will call me up to join him,
Together we will sing.

I hope today will be the day,
I won't have to pay,
I will love him every day.

Kirstin Hinton-Clark (11)
The Downs School, Newbury

Prize Roses

The world is like a garden
And we are the prize roses,
Well cared for,
Well watered,
In the good soil,
In the sunlight,
Life is perfect.
Put in designer vases
On the window;
See the world.

Poor people in the corner,
They are unwanted weeds,
Badly cared for,
No water,
In bad soil,
In the shadow.
Some with beautiful flowers,
Some with exquisite scents,
Some lying clipped and murdered on the ground,
Short-sighted gardeners poisoning them,
Always on the back of people,
Get rid of them or leave them?
Never been able to show their beauty,
They have been killed first.
The world is like a garden.

Sarah Hanson (11)
The Downs School, Newbury

Think If?

Think if the world had no poverty,
No war and no fights,
That's why I'm writing this poem,
To stand up for what I feel is right.

Think of the world with no racism,
No rivalry between blacks and whites,
The world would be so much more peaceful,
Without any more fights.

Think of the world where we could express ourselves,
With no one saying if we're right or wrong,
Where we could express ourselves
By stories, writing or by song.

Think if the world was peaceful,
Where everyone could find
A place in their heart to forgive those who have done wrong,
And be friendly to the ones who are kind.

Hannah Burnham (11)
The Downs School, Newbury

Accepting Me

Look at me
Sitting in my chair,
Nobody sees me,
Nobody cares.

I can't walk
And I can't run,
But I can think
And I can talk.

I feel like I am invisible,
Yet everyone can see me.
They sometimes point and stare
Or ignore me altogether.

I used to be like them,
Able to walk and run and play,
Feel the sand between my toes
And paddle in the sea,

Walk amongst the daisies in the fields
And go swimming in the pool,
Play football with my mates
Or go skating down the park.

Now all I can do is sit,
Sit and watch the world go by,
People coming and going,
Children laughing and joking.

Mum makes me go out
Now and again.
Every time I go,
I feel people's eyes follow me.

People's eyes do watch me
And make sure that I notice
Them laughing at me,
It makes me sick with anger.

I used to worry about hay fever,
Or not doing my maths homework,
But now those things don't matter,
Those silly little things.

I can't go to school
Because they don't accept me.
They laugh and joke
And call me names.

Why won't the world accept me?
Accept me for who I am,
Not judge me on my disability.
Just treat me for who I am.

Maisie Dawkes (13)
Windsor Girls' School, Windsor

Never 'Two' Young

(Dedicated to Gwyneth Hopkins)

They think I don't understand what's happening,
They think I cannot see,
They think I don't know about my fading memory.

There's a girl sitting next to me
With laughter in her eyes,
There's something in her touch that I recognise.

I know her scent,
I know her smile,
Maybe it'll come to me in a while.

A fire of frustration burns inside,
I know, I just know that she's on my side.

Something I can't put my finger on,
I don't know where I know her from.

I look at my reflection, so old and sickly,
It feels that my youth was over so quickly.

She kisses my cheek softly and whispers goodbye,
I watch her leave with a long, sad sigh.

The nurse comes over with two cups of tea
And puts them down next to me.
She turns towards me, I hear her say,
'Has your granddaughter gone? I hoped she'd stay.'

Bryony Hopkins (13)
Windsor Girls' School, Windsor

They Look At Me Like I'm Different

They look at me like I'm different,
Like I'm some kind of freak,
But I'm the same as them,
They're just to shallow to see.

They look at me like I'm different,
Hate is in their eyes,
I find it hard to see
Why it's me that they despise.

They look at me like I'm different,
Just because of my colour,
We're the same inside,
My personality is no duller.

They look at me like I'm different,
Because my skin is black,
But I would never change it,
It's just respect they lack.

They look at me like I'm different,
The feeling that it gives me,
It makes me feel so empty,
Why can't they leave me be!

They look at me like I'm different,
But if we turned out the light,
We wouldn't see a difference,
We wouldn't see black and white.

They look at me like I'm different,
They should open their eyes,
Take a look around them,
Why can't they hear my cries?

They look at me like I'm different,
But I'm proud to be what I am,
In truth there is no difference,
Like I said, I am what I am!

Ellie Cross (14)
Windsor Girls' School, Windsor

Ageism

Thinking of all the past memories,
Each one acting like a special key,
Unlocking the memories of the roads I took,
All my life now transferred into a book.

The days of my childhood seem so long ago,
But the years that have passed went everything but slow.
The years took their toll,
Taking the life out of my soul,
But still I sit here and smile,
Even though I feel fragile.

I sometimes feel alone, without anyone to talk to,
Not a person to share my thoughts, both old and new.
Why am I treated as I was in my youngest years?
Unable to be free but locked up with my fears.
I can't get outside or be in the open,
No one understands that I am still coping.
They all think I'm old
And do everything I'm told.

Just because I'm not always there,
It doesn't mean that I don't care,
So please be patient with me when I'm slow,
My memories may be somewhere else you know.

Do not be a judge of me
For there is more of me to see.
The outside tells a different tale,
I am strong, I am not frail.

Katrina Lally (13)
Windsor Girls' School, Windsor

You Are Prejudice

If you look you will see
People staring at you,
Staring at me,
With the black abyss of hate in your eyes,
You are Prejudice.

Don't think I haven't seen you looking,
Waiting for me to trip up,
To stumble,
To get down on my knees because you think you're superior,
You are Prejudice.

You think everyone's behind you,
Backing you up
With their fake laughs,
But I know they have pity in their hearts,
But not for me, for you.
You are Prejudice.

Some do have hate spread across their faces,
But when they curse and swear, they look at you.
Some feel sorrow, some pity, some hate,
But not for me for you.
You are Prejudice.

You bully me because I'm different,
They may have felt dislike towards me at first,
But they got over it, moved on.
You, however, are indifferent to my hurt.
I may seem to bruise easily on the surface,
But inside you are making me stronger.
You are Prejudice.

Bethany Laven (13)
Windsor Girls' School, Windsor

Bullying Is A Crime!

All my thoughts are locked within,
Waiting for a key,
Waiting for someone to tell them to,
I wait beneath the tree.

Cold and damp I sit alone,
Waiting for a friend,
No one wants to play with me,
I've got no one to befriend.

I watch them running, having fun,
Waiting for an invite.
I want to look like all of them,
I want my skin to look right.

They call me names, they shout and point,
Waiting for me to cry.
But I never do, I don't give in,
I keep my watered eyes dry.

Home time comes and I am free,
Waiting for my mum,
But she takes one look and she can see,
She knows what I've become.

I know I'll soon have to tell her,
Waiting for the time,
They cannot get away with this,
Bullying is a crime.

Rianne Payne (14)
Windsor Girls' School, Windsor

OAP

Nobody sees me
As I walk past with my stick
In my old-fashioned clothes
I won't part with.
The days go so slowly
As I wait for the end,
Away from this life I find lonely.

I wish I was young
And like you again,
With my whole life ahead of me.
I wish every loved one and family member
Was still living here with me.

It makes me sad to think
That the whole of my life
Can be summed up so easily.
I hang on to the past
In this world full of youth,
As there seems no future for me.

Jasmine Cheesewright (13)
Windsor Girls' School, Windsor